THE DIARY OF CONNIE SHAKESPEAR

THE NAGA HILLS 1900-1902

Edited by Nigel Shakespear

THE HIGHLANDER

THE HIGHLANDER

http://www.highlanderpress.org

Highlander Press
The Highland Institute
Meluri Road, Kohima Village
Kohima, Nagaland 797003

© 2021 Nigel Shakespear
© 2021 Highlander Press

The text of this book is licensed under a Creative Commons Attribution-NonCommercial-NoDerivatives 4.0 International license (CC BY-NC-ND 4.0). This license allows you to share, copy, distribute and transmit the work for non-commercial purposes, providing attribution is made to the author (but not in any way that suggests that he/she endorses you or your use of the work). **Attribution should include the following information:**

Shakespear, C. The Diary of Connie Shakespear: The Naga Hills 1900-1902. Edited and compiled by Nigel Shakespear. Kohima: Highlander Press, 2021

To access detailed and updated information on the license, please visit
http://www.highlanderpress.org
Further details about CC BY-NC-ND licenses are available at
https://creativecommons.org/licenses/by-nc-nd/4.0/

ISBN: 978-0-578-89046-3
LCCN: 2021936535

Cover design and layout by Alina Ronghangpi and Rokovor Vihienuo

CONTENTS

Map of Naga Hills		4
List of Illustrations		5
Name Changes		11
Glossary and Abbreviations		12
List of Characters		15
Foreword		17
Introduction		21
Chapter 1.	Tour to Henema, May 1900	33
Chapter 2.	Tour to Tamlu, July – August 1900	49
Chapter 3.	Journey to Manipur, September 1900	83
Chapter 4.	To Khonoma, October 1900	93
Chapter 5.	Tour to Kekrima and Mao Thana, December 1900	101
Chapter 6.	Tour to Mokokchung, January 1901	119
Chapter 7.	Kohima and Dimapur, February 1901	151
Chapter 8.	Kohima and Christmas Tour, December 1901	169
Chapter 9.	Kohima, January 1902	189
Chapter 10.	Tour to Tamlu, February 1902	201
Bibliography		229
Constance Mackworth Shakespear – A Short Biography		233
Editor's Note		235

NAGA HILLS 1900 – 1902

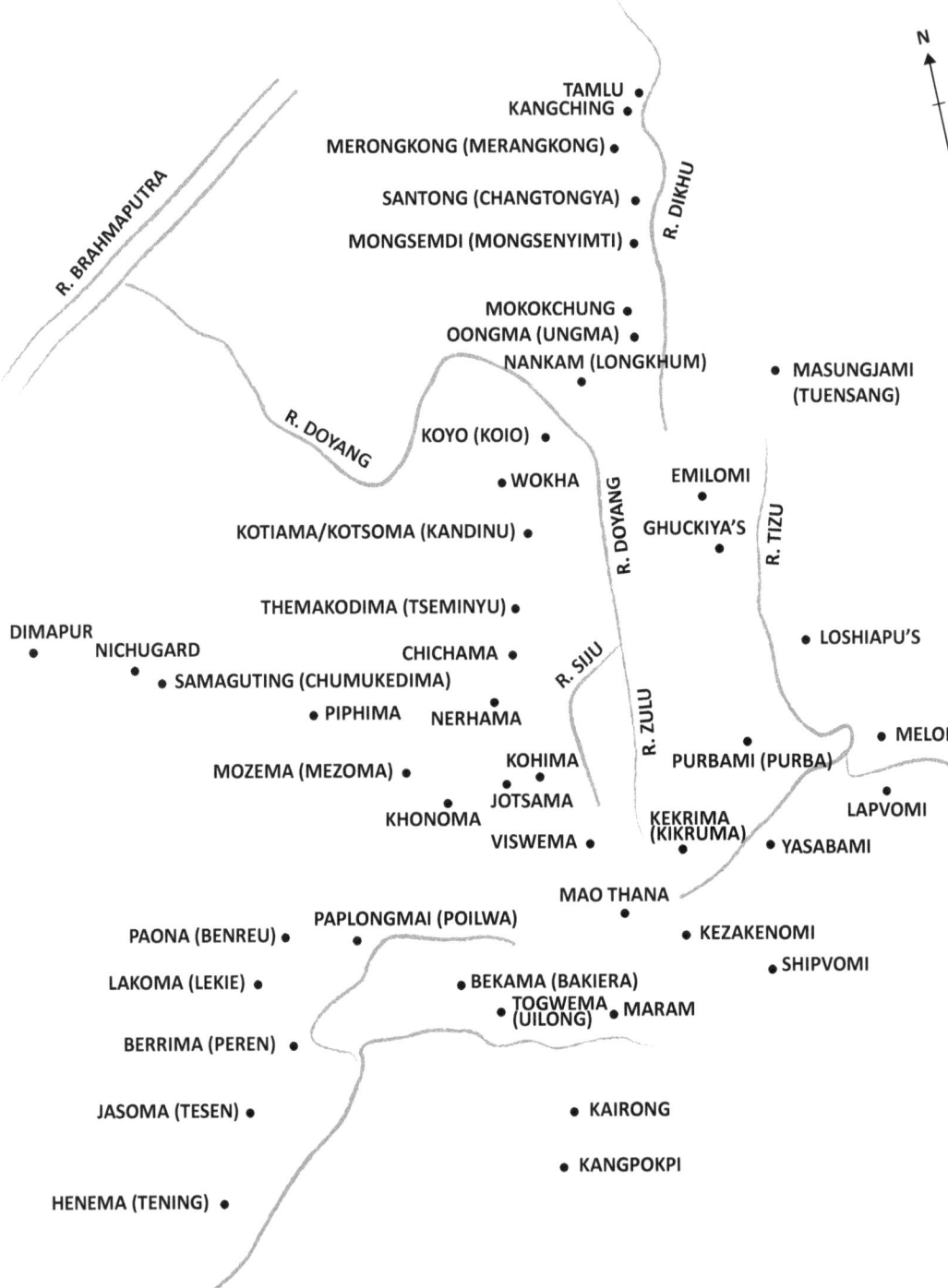

ILLUSTRATIONS

Page 22	Diary notebooks
Page 25	A page from a notebook
Page 32	'Carved gate at Jotsoma' May 1900
Page 34	'Khonoma' May 1900
Page 34	'Paona Rest House El. 8100' ' May 1900
Page 36	'Berrima village'
Page 36	'Rest house and earthwork fort Henema Kacha Naga country'
Page 37	'Entrance to Henema fort'
Page 37	'Henema village' May 1900
Page 38	'Kacha Naga village of Duphima near Henema'
Page 39	Untitled – dancing
Page 40	'A ballet at Henema by Kaccha men and women' May 1900
Page 41	Untitled – dancers
Page 41	Untitled – dancers
Page 42	Untitled – dancers
Page 42	Henema, May 1900
Page 43	'Principle dancers' May 1900
Page 44	'Street in Henema Kaccha Naga'
Page 44	Henema, May 1900
Page 45	'Jasoma'
Page 46	'Paona'
Page 48	'Tamsi of Nankam' 1900
Page 51	'Pochiris from Melomi'
Page 53	'Carved tree trunks at Koyo'
Page 55	'Corner in Nankum Village, Aoh Nagas, July 1900'
Page 56	Untitled – village
Page 56	'In Nankam village' 1900
Page 57	'View of Mokokchang'
Page 59	'Mongsemdi stockade Aoh Naga country'
Page 60	'A village orator - Santong village (Aoh)' 1900
Page 61	'LWS and Noel Williamson at Tamlu'
Page 61	'Santong', log drum 1900
Page 63	'Merankong village from above' 1900
Page 63	'Corner in Merangkong, Aoh village, showing how the houses are supported' 1900

Page 64	Untitled
Page 66	'Tamlu stockade'
Page 68	'Tamlu. Moranghur' August 1900
Page 69	'Io/Ayo and Impi', Tamlu August 1900
Page 71	'Trans-Dikku Nagas at Merankong. Group of Lengta Naga' 1900
Page 73	'Mongsemdi stockade' August 1900
Page 75	'Headmen at Masungjami'
Page 76	'Corner in the Aoh Naga village of Nankam Miss Ingram taking a photo' August 1900
Page 77	'Luntiang rest house El 4000' '
Page 79	'Con and Miss Ingram at Kotsoma'
Page 82	'Deputy Commissioner's house and garden' Kohima
Page 84	'Japoli our Naga malli in rain hat and grass cloak. (Phesama village)'
Page 85	'Squads volley firing Tesima Range 500 yds'
Page 87	'Genna stones at Maram'
Page 89	'The Tikki river - Kaithenmanbi'
Page 90	'Graves of Melville and O'Brien cut up by Nagas in /91 Mayonkong'
Page 91	'Doorga Pooja fete' Manipur, September 1900
Page 92	'Our sitting room' Kohima, 1900
Page 94	'Near Khonoma'
Page 96	'Khonoma "Club", November 1900
Page 97	'Look out post - Khonoma Fort'
Page 97	'Magazine in Khonoma fort'
Page 98	'Khonoma fort north corner entrance. Barail Range in the distance'
Page 100	'Graves at Kekrima - nearer view of graves' 1900
Page 102	'Terraced cultivation'
Page 103	'Con being carried across the Sijoo River, between Kezuma and Kekrima'
Page 104	'Our camp in Kekrima village', December 1900
Page 105	'View in Kekrima village when we sketched E. Angamis' December 1900
Page 105	'Warriors graves shield representation of heads taken by the departed' Dec 1900

Page 106	'View in Kekrima village E. Angami' December 1900
Page 107	'Building (repairing) a house in Kekrima' December 1900
Page 109	'Tekobarma E.Angami Village belle' December 1900
Page 109	'Narkuma' December 1900
Page 110	'Nisami Kezami Nagas' December 1900
Page 111	'Nisami Kezami Nagas' December 1900
Page 111	'Village water supply. Cherama. Kezami Nagas' December 1900
Page 112	'Cherama' December 1900
Page 113	'Cherama Dhan pounding festival Kezami Nagas' December 1900
Page 114	'On path between Kezakenoma and Mao Thana'
Page 115	'View on road from Kezakanoma to Mao' December 1900
Page 115	'Genna stones at Mao Thana' December 1900
Page 116	'Kapani's house at Mao Thana' December 1900
Page 116	'On road from Jakoma to Kohima' December 1900
Page 117	'Kapani, headman of Mao' December 1900
Page 118	'Mithun and group at Ghuckia's' January 1901
Page 121	Ms Ingram and CMS in village
Page 123	'Sataka bungalow after the fire' 13 January 1901
Page 124	'Headman at Jekia's village – Sema Nagas'
Page 125	'Sema Nagas at Jekia's village'
Page 127	'Chief's House Ghukia's Village N Sema Nagas'
Page 128	'Ghuckia's village'
Page 129	'Emilomi'
Page 130	'Emilomi village El. 6000'
Page 130	'Lhoshiapu - Sema chief'
Page 132	Untitled
Page 133	'Lota warrior charging'
Page 134	'Lemomi Rest house'
Page 135	'Mokok'
Page 137	'Mokok'
Page 138	'Nankum'
Page 139	'War Drum, Nunkum'
Page 140	'Namkum Moranghurs, or Club houses, for the young men'
Page 140	'Corner in Lungtiang Village (Sema)'
Page 141	'Lungtyan Sema'
Page 141	'Doyang bridge'

Page 142	'Wokha fort'
Page 143	'Temakodima' bungalow
Page 144	'Temakodima' village
Page 145	'Mithun and group in Themakodima village (Rengma)'
Page 145	'Mithun speared for a feast'
Page 146	'Wokha Post Office' January 1901
Page 147	Wokha Post Office burnt down' January 1901
Page 148	'Temakodima Guason'
Page 149	'Tesima bungalow'
Page 149	'Our house Kohima'
Page 150	'Kohima warrior in festal dress. Feathers of the tail of the Toucan'.
Page 151	'Kohima from the gate'
Page 152	'Sibboo our cook and Japoli in their war paint. (Samaguting village)'. Kohima
Page 153	'Entrance to our house, Manipur cart road to right'
Page 154	'In front of our house. Sibboo, wife, wife's friend, his boy. Our servants' houses'
Page 155	'Kohima village'
Page 155	'Dhan (rice) pounding festival Kohima' 1901
Page 156	'Dhan (rice) pounding festival Kohima' 1901
Page 157	'Dhan (rice) pounding festival Kohima' 1901
Page 157	'Angami Nagas pounding rice in full war paint at the Dhan pounding festival' Kohima
Page 158	'Dhan (rice) pounding festival Kohima' 1901
Page 159	'Angami interpreters' Nihu in centre
Page 159	'Cart road near Piphima' 1901
Page 160	'Ghaspani – Rest house' February 1901
Page 161	'Kuki Pani bridge' February 1901
Page 161	'Nichuguard – Rest House' February 1901
Page 162	'Dimapur Tank – and bungalow' February 1901
Page 162	'Dunsiri river at Dimapur' February 1901
Page 163	'Ancient monoliths in the ruined fort at Dimapur.' February 1901
Page 164	Dimapur Cachari monolith 1901
Page 165	'Entrance to ancient fort at Dimapur (Cachari)' 1901
Page 165	'Monolith discovered at Dimapur - conjectured at 2000 years old'.

Page 166   'Gauhati Dak bungalow' February 1901
Page 166   'Steamers on the Brahmaputra' Gauhati February 1901
Page 168   'Angami warrior' Kohima
Page 170   'Guard house. S. end of Khonoma fort'
Page 171   'Kohima, Nagas dancing on parade ground'
Page 172   'Angami in gala attire', Kohima
Page 173   'Kekrima, 24.12.01'
Page 174   'Chaboma 25.12.01'
Page 175   'Razema 26.12.01'
Page 176   'Halt by the way on road between Razema and Thetchilumi'
Page 177   'Thetchilumi' December 1901
Page 177   'Thetchilumi' December 1901
Page 178   'Thetchilumi 27.12.01'
Page 179   'Corner in Kezabama Eastern Angami 28.12.01'
Page 180   'Kezabama' December 1901
Page 181   'Purbami' December 1901
Page 182   'Purbami' December 1901
Page 183   'Chadoma'
Page 184   'Angami Naga house in Chadoma village – weaving in front of house'
Page 185   'Below Chadoma' December 1901
Page 186   'Bridge over Sijoo River EL. 2400'
Page 186   CMS, Captain and Mrs. Bliss
Page 187   'Naga Rest House near Kohima 1901'
Page 187   'Near Kohima 31.12.01'
Page 188   'Phaius Wallichii'
Page 190   Wyn, in cadet uniform at school in England
Page 191   '44th G.R. lines from our garden'
Page 192   LWS
Page 194   'N.H.M.P. orderly room and recruits parade'
Page 195   'Kohima visits Phesama'
Page 196   'N.H.M.P. on parade'
Page 197   'Con and the Mirris'
Page 200   'Moimang and Io/Ayo, Lengta Nagas, Tamlu' February 1902
Page 202   'Grave Chichama N. Angami Feb 6th 1902'
Page 203   'Grave of a village notable Temakodima 6 Feb 1902'
Page 204   'Lhota Naga grave', 6 February 1902

Page 204   'Graves at Themakodima - Rengma Nagas' February 1902
Page 205   'Lhota woman weaving'
Page 205   Sema warriors'
Page 206   'Sema Naga in war paint'
Page 206   'Sema Naga in war paint'
Page 207   ''Lhota woman'
Page 209   'Aohs carving a tree trunk'
Page 210   'Aoh Naga grave'
Page 211   'Street in an Aoh Naga village'
Page 212   'An Aoh Naga'
Page 212   'Tamlu 16.2.02' Morang
Page 213   'Tamlu village'
Page 213   'Daupan and his heads'
Page 214   'Skulls & children's bodies in the burial tree'
Page 216   'Skulls at foot of tree' Tamlu, February 1902
Page 217   'Wuang a Lengta Naga of Tamlu', February 1902
Page 218   'Moimang, Tablungias, Daupan' and Io
Page 218   'Tamlu morang upper Khel'
Page 220   'Morang in Kanching'
Page 220   'Lanoo our dobasha from Merangkong and coolies en route to Santong'
Page 222   'Group of NHMP officers at entrance to Mokokchung fort' February 1902
Page 222   'Subedar Arjun Rai and family' February 1902
Page 223   'Ungma village'
Page 223   'A death in the house', Nankam
Page 224   'The bathing pool at Wokha'
Page 225   'Bindong' February 1902
Page 226   'Themakodima – Rengma Nagas'
Page 227   'Gwasen and his protege J.M.'

CHANGES TO NAMES OF PLACES IN THE DIARY

DIARY NAME	MODERN NAME
Bekama	Bakiera
Berrima	Peren
Bor Tablung	Wanching
Gohati/Gauhati	Guwahati
Henema	Tening
Jasoma	Tesen
Kanching	Kangching
Kekrima	Kikruma
Kotiama/Kotsoma	Kandinu
Koyo	Koio
Lakoma	Lekie
Longtak	Loktak
Manipur	Imphal, capital of Manipur state
Masungjami	Tuensang
Merongkong	Merangkong
Mongsemdi	Mongsemyimti
Mozema	Mezoma
Nambur	Nambor forest in the Brahmaputra plain
Nankam/Nunkum/Lungkum (stone birth)	Longkhum
Paplongmai/Kenema	Poilwa
Paona	Benreu
Purbami	Purba
Samaguting	Chumukedima
Santong/Chantung	Changtongya
Themakodima/Temekodima	Tseminyu
Togwema	Uilong
Uhngma/Oongma/Uongma	Ungma (burnt down and rebuilt in 1901)

GLOSSARY AND ABBREVIATIONS

Babu	Indian clerk
Cacha or Katcha Naga	This term covers both Zeme and Zeliang
C.C.	Chief Commissioner for Assam, based in Shillong
Chaukidar/Chowkidar	watchman (in this case looking after bungalows)
Chunga	bamboo container or storage vessel
Dak	the postal system, or mail. Bungalows on bridle paths were rest houses or 'dak' bungalows.
D.C.	Deputy Commissioner
Dhan	rice
Dao/dhao	flat bladed, heavy duty all-purpose knife or chopper
Dobasha – dobashi	interpreter
Dog-cart	light horse-drawn vehicle
Eastern Angami	Chakhesang
Goanbura	Gaonbura, headman of a village
Genna stones	stones, megaliths and erected monuments, of mythological and social significance
Ghurrah	earthenware pot
Gladstone	bag
Goorkhin/Gurkhin	female Goorkha/Gurkha (possibly a personal term used by CMS)
Havildar	native soldier's rank equating to a sergeant
Homadriad	Hamadryad or King Cobra
Hooluk	Hoolock Gibbon
Independent country	territory occasionally visited by the British which was not under their control

Jemadar	native officer rank equating to Lieutenant
Jhapa	basket with a lid
Jooming	jhooming/jhuming, burning land in slash-and-burn agriculture
Job's Tears	crop, *(Coix lachryma-jobi)*
Khel	area/quarter/ward of a village usually associated with one clan and its sub-divisions
Khit	servant role
Khud race	race up and then down a steep hill, at which Gurkhas excel
Kutcheri	public office for administrative or judicial business: courthouse
Lengta Naga	Phom/Konyak
Lines	soldiers' barracks
Machan	platform set up in a tree
Mess	the officers' clubhouse
Mitton	Mithun *(Bos frontalis)* or gayal, a large bovine animal with massive horns
Morunghar/Morung	place of education for young men (or women) which was also their dormitory providing a guard force for immediate defence
M.P.	Military Police
N.H.M.P.	Naga Hills Military Police
Panji	short pointed stake of hardened bamboo stuck in the ground to impede enemy progress
Political Control Country	the buffer zone between British administered land and the 'Independent country', in which villages paid no tax and were not afforded protection but raiding was forbidden and violent crimes such as murder were punished

PMO	Principal Medical Officer
POP	Printing-out paper: a photographic paper
Puja/Pooja	worship ritual
Purdah	screen, veil or curtain
Purdah nashin	woman who observes purdah
PWD	Public Works Department, part of the British administration
Sambhur	deer
Sarametti	highest mountain in the Naga Hills
Sattar	sitar
Sconce	candle holder that is attached to a wall with an ornamental bracket
S.D.O.	Sub-divisional Officer
Sealdah	a railway terminus in Calcutta
Sepoy	soldier
Subedar	native officer rank equating to Captain
Subedar Major	native officer rank equating to Major
Tamasha	grand show or performance
Tiffin	lunch or light midday meal
Tonga	light carriage drawn by one horse
Tonkal	Tangkhul
Topper	or topha – porter's basket to carry a person on the back
Toucan	Hornbill
Tumtum	local word for a dog-cart, a light horse-drawn vehicle
Zu	rice beer

LIST OF CHARACTERS

The Naga Villagers

Chadoma	Lohoki the dobasha
Gukia	Gukia the gaonbura
Jaetong	Jaetong the gaonbura
Jekia's village	Jekia the gaonbura
Kohima	Viletia; Nihu, dobasha, later a signatory of the Naga Memorandum
Mao Thana	Kapani the gaonbura; Ahtika
Merongkong (Merangkong)	Lanu the dobasha; Molong the gaonbura
Nankam (Longkhum)	Tumsi the dobasha; Bindong, wife of the second dobasha; Alum Khaber/Kabi the chowkidar
Santong (Changtongya)	Monti the gaonbura
Sataka	Sataka the gaonbura
Susu	Panchong Lambar
Tamlu	Daupan; Wang the 'mistri'; Moimang the dobasha; Ayo/Io and Impi; Tablungias
Themakodima (Tseminyu)	Guason the gaonbura and Johnny (his son?)

The British and Others

Kohima, military: 44th Gurkha Rifles - Colonel Molesworth, Mr. George Ward, Humphries, Sergeant Dorward, Mr. Melvill Inspector of Signalling

Kohima, N.H.M.P: LWS, Sergeant W.E. Tolley, Subedar Sonjai/Sinjai/Sonjai Suba (a Gurkha), Jemadar Wazira (a Dogra), Jemadar Belbong Rana, Subedar Rajobin/Ragobin (a Garhwali), Subedar Jamaluddin, Jemadar Ziaram/Tia Ram, Jemadar Dayaram/Diaram (a Garhwali), Subedar Karti Ram/Katiram

Kohima, political and admin: Captain Woods D.C., Captain Kennedy Assistant Commissioner, Captain Somerset DAQG, Major and Mrs. Kerr, Major Charles and Mrs. Bliss, Mr. Grant, Mr. Nightingale Chief Engineer, Mr. Knight, Mr. Pritchard, Dr. Weinman, Mr. Daniell, Eardley Wilmot, Mr. White, Dr. and Mrs. Willmore, Assistant Surgeon (native) and Scotch wife

Kohima, missionaries: Dr. and Mrs. Rivenberg

Kohima, servants and staff: Assimoo, Hooli, Sibboo the cook, Sibboo's boy Kulu, Massadi the khit, Miltu the Naga assistant khit, Japali the mali or gardener, Hira Singh, Hosiaru, Ino Ram the orderly

Wokka: Pompa Sing the new Deputy Collector, N.H.M.P. Havildar Tulsi, Jadob Binda the Post Office clerk.

Mokokchung: Sub Divisional Officer (SDO) Noel Williamson; N.H.M.P. Subedar Major Arjun Rai (a Gurkha)

Tamlu: N.H.M.P. Jemadar Bakshi

Dimapur: Surgeon Colonel Dr. Cave-Calthrop, Dr. Leventon

Manipur/Imphal: Tom Hodson Assistant Political Agent, Colonel Maxwell, Bagleys 3rd Bengal Infantry, Mr. Langhorn Sub PWD

Connie's family and friends: Wyn – her son, Tom Biddulph – her brother and Lil her sister in law, Miss Ingram or B. – a lady companion during Connie's first visit to Nagaland.

Foreword

Reading the private thoughts of an unsuspecting person makes one feel somewhat guilty, despite knowing that the person in question is long deceased. Such a feeling is quickly dispensed with when we read the diary of Connie Shakespear as we come to realise that it may well become a document of historical importance for the Nagas, of whom she writes about.

The introduction states that this journal/diary covers a period time of which we do not have much knowledge. As things stand, we do not have any written record of that time from the indigenous people's point of view and therefore it would be prudent for us to accept the document for what it is – a historical document. Connie was neither a proselyte nor an adventuress. She was the wife of a British officer in the Indian army. She would probably have never come to the Naga Hills had not her husband been posted there. She was a 'normal' housewife who acted, thought and wrote as was expected from a person of her class and time. It is vital to know the place she comes from or the position she occupies, to understand why she uses terms like 'savages' or 'barbaric' to describe the indigenous people she comes in contact with. To be carried atop a 'topper' was a privilege that was accorded to her which she seems to have received without any hesitation. The modern reader, especially a Naga reader, may well forgive her keeping in mind Apostle Paul's words in Acts 17: 30... "The times of ignorance God overlooked, but now he commands all people everywhere to repent" which, in this context, may be paraphrased to mean that we may overlook the actions borne out of ignorance in olden times, but now people who have committed such actions should change their mindsets for the better and heartily amend their ways with abhorrence for their past actions. And this holds true not only for our erstwhile colonial masters but also for those of us in the present generation as we witness the many forms of discrimination that still exists all over the world.

Once we get past the differences in approaches to life, we will be able to appreciate the information that she provides through her entries, with the sketches and photographs that accompany them. There are a good number of photographs and a few sketches which are undoubtedly the USP of the book. The photos that evoke the most excitement in me are those of "Nankam" or "Lungtum" because I believe these are of Longkhum, the village I belong to – the clues being provided in the description of the village and in the map. The sketches are lifelike, though few in number. There are pictures of morungs, graves, natives in traditional attires, the camps and landscape. These pictures help bridge the gap between the imagination of the reader and reality that was. They also bring alive the vast cultural differences between the writer and those written about.

The beauty and rich natural world of the Naga Hills are depicted in many entries as well. There are multiple entries on butterflies (though we may no longer approve of the method of collecting them). Wildlife hunting was an acceptable sport, and game meat was relished while wild animals were given as gifts and kept as pets. The picturesque landscape never fails to amaze her. Leslie, her husband, is apparently very much at home in the mountains, gazing up the clear night skies whenever time permitted. The first chapter talks of a "glorious day and the Forest most lovely." She mentions tall, white lilies; wonderful plants with huge leaves as tall as her husband with marvellous blossoms rising from the root, as well as ferns and orchids. Many beautiful plants and orchids are collected during their treks. One wonders whether some made it to England and flourished there, and if seeds and saplings were brought and introduced to the Naga Hills.

We read of a village in the Sema country called "Lemoni" where the people made clay "ghurrahs" which were used instead of the wooden and bamboo vessels used by other tribes; about a belief among the Semas of a fabled place in Burma where only women live and from where no man has ever returned from; freshly tattooed young Ao girls; a women's market in Manipur (which still exists); inter-racial marriages (in Chapter 9, we find mention of a "native" Assistant Surgeon with a Scotch wife, an officer named Jamaluddin married to a Naga and the senior Gurkha officer Arjun Rai is married to an Angami Naga) – anecdotes which might interest readers. Though generally unimpressed by Naga looks and lack of hygiene, she appreciates traits like generosity and good temper that she notices in the people, highlighting one incident where children willingly share fruit without a murmur.

She also allows herself to become a 'specimen' to be observed by the curious natives and is quite sporting about it, livening up her entries with touches of dry humour, especially in her interactions with the natives who find the sight of a 'lady' a novelty. Instances of such indulgences are evidenced when she shows them her uncovered hands and feet. She and her troupe eat in front of the whole village, much like performing a play! That she had no interest in assimilating the natives into the 'mainstream' is evident in her description of a fellow named Jaetong who wore some clothing items presented by "some misguided missionary" which she writes, was "such a shame to have turned so fine a fellow into such a guy."

One fellow who she finds equally amusing and exasperating is Ayoh/Ayo/Io (she is rather lax in her spelling and uses different variants for the same person or place) who being quite the ladies' man, appears to have proposed to both Connie and her friend, Miss Ingram, despite the barrier in language. This in spite of the fact that he had a bride with whom he had recently eloped! This comical episode in Chapter 2, is most entertaining and one can't help but admire the supreme confidence of the man, and the incongruity of the situation brought alive by Connies's witty rendering of it.

What about the women? We have Connie, a *memsahib* of the Empire, writing about the indigenous women and the wives of the native officers, quite a rare occurrence in itself. Apart from some passing comments on the women in the villages that she meets during her travels, and some observations on Impi, the bride of the "great" Ayo, the women in the station in Kohima are the ones she describes in some detail. Station life and its peculiar courtesies are highlighted in Chapter 9, when she and Mrs. Tolley go visiting the wives of the native officers and are obliged to sit and eat over and over again in all the houses. The women are always referred to by their husband's names and she doesn't seem to have become close to any one of them. Mrs. Jamaluddin is a Naga and speaks some Hindi. She is described as a nice, pleasant woman more than once and seems more confident than the rest. Two Gharwali women, Mrs. Rajobin, who has five children, and Mrs. Diaram, are both described as very pretty. Mrs. Sonjai/Sunjai is a pure Gurkhin/Goorkin who is unable to speak any language apart from her native tongue. The wife of Wazira the Dogra is not only very pretty but highly ornamented and very shy. Due to her extreme shyness, the husband takes over the duty of entertaining the visitors.

This series of interactions with different women takes almost the whole day and tires Connie. She is more enthusiastic about her treks than these social visits. One cannot help but notice that there is a substantial cultural divide between her and the wives of the native officers, the only common ground being talk of their respective children.

Today, as I introspect on her life as depicted in the diary, there are areas I can relate to – like her focus on action and getting work done and dislike for small talk. I also admire the way she tackles trekking despite her bulky attire. Connie in her Victorian corset and hat traipsing around thick jungle must have been quite a sight! She had to deal with societal conventions but managed to take time out to enjoy herself. Her life is definitely easier by the presence of many servants, a luxury many of us cannot afford nowadays. Living apart from her husband for long periods of time, and with her son Wyn in boarding school, she probably had the leisure to practise music and painting and other hobbies.

She seems to be in good health, for she walks long distances (whenever she is not being carried) over jungle terrain. She mentions names of people and places in the spellings that were current at the time of writing, gives geographical and ethnographical details along with dates. Hopefully, these pointers will enable scholars to decipher and add notes in the years to come. It is my belief that genuine scholars will be interested in this book and what it has to offer. After all, it is always preferable to encounter depictions of past history in stark black and white, both literally and figuratively, rather than believe the whitewashed ones that are being increasingly touted nowadays.

A. Sentiyula
Assistant Professor, Dimapur Government College

Introduction

Whether in her mind this was a diary or a travel journal, for sure Connie Shakespear never thought her writing was going to be published. Most diaries aren't written for publication, yet there's often a reader over the writer's shoulder. Poor Connie! She would never have imagined it might be you, dear reader. May she forgive me!

So why publish? In a time of calls for the decolonisation of history this diary might be seen as mere jottings from a colonial notebook, a repetition of what we know already as well as something undesirable from the imperial attic. Also there's no claim her writing is of deep literary appeal although it's fair to say she writes well, avoids the dramatic, provides vivid sketches and takes you with her on her journeys. No, the value of this short text is in its timing and the photography. The diary is a document that includes personal photographs, an early one of its kind, illustrating the experience of both British and indigenous subjects in the Naga Hills at the turn of the 20th century. At this time the politically turbulent Naga Hills under British control had been pacified while most of the traditional village culture remained – the great social and cultural changes brought about by the Baptist missions had yet to come. This is primary source material covering a specific period in a specific place, too valuable to be left in the attic.

Constance Mackworth Shakespear was married to Captain Leslie W. Shakespear of the Indian Army. LWS had been appointed Commandant of the Naga Hills Military Police in 1897. He remained there five years, based in the hill station of Kohima, and in that time Connie visited him twice, arriving first in December 1899. On this occasion she brought with her a lady com-

panion, a Miss Ingram. In all she was 19 months in the Naga Hills and during that time she accompanied LWS as he travelled on some of his duty tours in the district, recording seven journeys in her diary.

This is no bureaucratic colonial record although she copies some elements from official tour diaries. It is a manuscript written in two A5 sized notebooks in which some small photographic prints were attached on hinged fastenings. Many of these have come adrift leaving hinge but no photo. Whilst being a personal diary there's nothing about herself in a work that sets about documenting their tours with information on the journey, the country, the villages, the people and their customs, as well as the NHMP. She also covers something of station life for the British in Kohima. This is the only writing of hers to survive – it seems likely she felt the value of it. Both she and LWS must have been well aware they were somewhere special, that it was worth recording, though there's no hint they thought the centuries old culture that surrounded them would change so drastically in the next hundred years.

The diary is part of an archive, an imperial archive, which also includes LWS' personal memoir and other documents, along with albums and more than a thousand photographs. All of these relate to the life of an Indian Army soldier. He was the author of five books including histories of North East India and of the Assam Rifles and took an active role in the British response to the Kuki rebellion of 1917-1918 in N.E. India. Their son later served in the Assam Rifles at Kohima. The archive has provided relevant contemporary photographs which fill those gaps in the diary.

Married to a representative of colonial power at the zenith of the British Empire in India, before Indian nationalism had really made itself felt, Connie is a Victorian 'memsahib', has a sense of entitlement and leads a privileged life in the Naga Hills. She takes for granted the servants who look after their bungalow or make their camp, cook their meals, collect their plants and look after their animals, as well as the porters or coolies who give her rides in a 'topper' and carry their kit. The life she leads and the way the world works to her advantage is not something she ever questions.

She sees herself at the 'furthest limits of civilisation' and the indigenous people as being uncivilized and backward. She would have seen herself, the English lady, as a superior being. After all, this is just three years after Queen Victoria's Diamond Jubilee and five years since Joseph Chamberlain, British Colonial Secretary, declared in a speech on 11 November 1895: "I believe in this race, the greatest governing race the world has ever seen; in this Anglo-Saxon race, so proud, tenacious, self-confident and determined, this race which neither climate nor change can degenerate, which will infallibly be the predominant force of future history and universal civilization."

So her diary is a colonial era document steeped in the language of imperialism and her attitude comes out in the writing. A dependant of a representative of the established power, she is a woman of her time, not ahead of her time. But she is also interested in the Naga people amongst whom she travels and she is a curious and observant person. She might see Naga villagers as uncivilized but she is able to appreciate them as people. As an observer she is not untouched by them. Sensitive to individuals whom she gets to know she provides small portraits of Nagas from her outsider's perspective. They can impress her. She can be appreciative, complimentary and generous in her comments on them: 'her house so nice and clean', 'a fine village', 'a nice looking delightful people', 'a gentleman', 'well-mannered' and so on. Some she feels are friends. But at the same time they are 'savages' which can be confusing for her.

As a writer her tone is undramatic, unemotional, matter-of-fact, objective. She employs irony and humour. She is straightforward and honest. When she likes something she says so, and when she doesn't she can be critical, especially when it comes to cleanliness. 'A miserable, low, dirty looking lot', comes to mind. But there's no scorn or contempt in her voice.

Born into an established British Indian family (Biddulph) and married into another, and eight years older than her husband, she exhibits a sense of place and class. At 48 years old she is completely at home in India yet shows a nostalgia for her mother country where her son is at school. She enjoys her 'dak' – the mail. She is an accomplished person in art, music and sports, she is able to travel distances over difficult terrain in her voluminous Victorian attire, she enjoys the musicality of the Naga people and she's able to appreciate a different culture and adapt. She makes no fuss and is amused by those that do, she shows respect where she feels it due, she is caring and she's not callous. She speaks no ill of people and makes fun only of the Indian 'babu', like so many of her kind. Again like them, when it came to class she was a snob, something which comes out on the ship returning home to England.

The monographs on the Naga tribes such as *The Angami* by J.H. Hutton, the British administrator, were not available to the two of them and there's no evidence Connie had read any of the earlier papers and books written on Nagas by Butler, Woodthorpe, Mackenzie or any other of the earlier colonial writers. On the inside of one of her diary books is the inscription: 'Anthropological Secretary, Asiatic Society of Bengal, 57 Park Street, Calcutta'. Does this indicate she was that person? She takes note of and comments on graves, dress, custom and 'court proceedings'; she records systematically the tribes amongst whom they pass (the classification of the people in the Naga Hills into tribes being a British construct) which suggests an interest in ethnology. It is clear though she had a knowledge of the colonial record and the conflict between the British and Naga peoples.

In the 19th century only a few European women had visited the Naga Hills. Colonial officials and soldiers had been in and out of the hills and a handful were accompanied by their wives. In 1851 Captain Vincent's wife joined him on a tour and Johnstone's wife lived with him in Samaguting near Dimapur where Butler had been stationed with his wife some 20 years earlier. In 1874 Polly Badgley went with her husband on a survey trip, climbing the mountain overlooking Kohima – now called Pulie Badze, Angami for 'Polly's Seat' according to LWS [not the current explanation]. In 1879 Mrs. Cawley

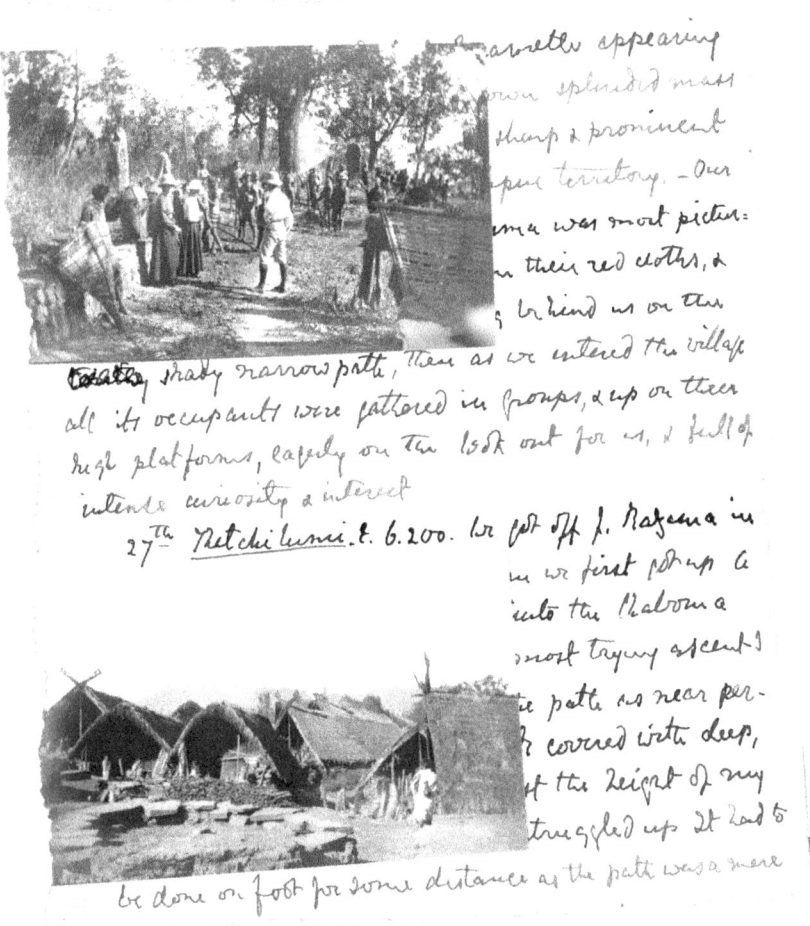

left an eye-witness report on the Angami siege of the British at Kohima. Ethel Grimwood, known for her account of the 1891 British disaster in Manipur, also preceded Connie, as did some other wives in Kohima in the 1880's and 90's. Apart from the British women there were also the American Baptist missionaries, notably Mary Mead Clark who in 1907 published a book on her experiences with the Nagas. With her husband she had lived 'beyond the British flag' in Molung in the Naga Hills from 1876. So Connie was not the first of European women to visit the Naga Hills nor was she the first to write about her experiences and her diary is short but the extensive use of a hand-held camera differentiates her work from the others. All four women writers mentioned above share a cool objectivity: they don't romanticize or dramatize.

The photographic record of Connie's journeys strengthens her written story. Eastman brought out the Kodak Brownie in 1900 and similar cameras had been around for some 10 years so the dawn of amateur photography was underway and the Shakespears played a part in this. LWS took photos in 1898 but their photography started seriously in 1900. Presumably untutored, they both had a sense of the aesthetic, a photographer's eye, and developed their own photographs from 2 ¼ x 3 ¼ inch negatives, of which none have survived. Some photographs were published later in his books while the rest were confined to personal albums, providing a wide-ranging window on their world. They took opportunities to photograph the vernacular, to illustrate their journeys, making a straight record for their own purposes of the life around them, standing back from the villagers as outside observers. While the reaction of some subjects give a hint of the colonial relationship there are no 'colonial subjects sitting for the colonial record'. A few photographs taken by LWS exhibit a documentary style suggesting a feeling for ethnographic record. Occasionally he stages a scene and in fact it is in the portraits taken in Tamlu that they come closest to the people of a village. The photographs are a source of information. Knowledgeable readers will be able to add to, comment on and perhaps correct information in the text.

So while this 'imperial' document exemplifies the colonial perspective and British attitudes it also provides a written and photographic record of Naga villages and their people at the turn of the 20th century. It comes between earlier 19th century British accounts, like those of Woodthorpe with his written material, water-colours and drawings, and the coming of the later well-known ethnographers like Hutton after 1910. The diary does not compare with the wealth of information, ideas and thinking about the Nagas found in these works but it does provide a tale of 'interaction' coupled with vernacular photography which make it significant.

The diary is published to open that window on this specific period. It is for specialists with an interest in history and anthropology. As a historical document it reflects the British mindset and attitude of the day. The publication is also for today's Naga descendants and those visiting Nagaland who want to take a look at the villages, people and country as they were just over a century ago. This is history from the British perspective. There is an unwritten history to be found in the villages where they travelled, villages with an oral culture which would tell another story. That Naga voice also deserves a hearing.

Connie wrote her manuscript in pen in her notebooks with very little amendment and few crossings-out or insertions, probably on the day in question. She uses abbreviations and occasionally her English can be a little rough and unpolished. Occasional grammatical errors can occur and sometimes there's a loss of sense. The spelling of place names and local people can be inconsistent, probably due to the phonetic provenance of these words. She also makes occasional errors of fact.

An unedited digital version of the diary, as close to the original manuscript as possible, is available at the Highland Institute website. This printed edition is only lightly edited, removing abbreviations and one egregious example of imperial statement about the local 'savages' for reasons of sensitivity. Spelling, grammar and mistakes remain untouched, so for example 'Toucan' remains Toucan – commonly misapplied by Europeans in British India to the 'Hornbill' – and Goanbura is not corrected to Gaonbura.

After she left the Naga Hills Connie had an article published in *The Wide World Magazine* in 1902. This was not passed down in the archive and has recently come to light. In this she covers her tour through the Sema country a year earlier, recounted in Chapter 6. The text follows that of her diary, sometimes word for word, sometimes rearranged, adjusted or elaborated, and while it omits some elements like the fire at Sataka it includes photographs and story not found in the diary or archive. The magazine, first published in 1898, tells of tales of derring-do, 'true-life' adventure and excitement. Unsurprisingly Connie's article, while presenting the Sema as in the diary, tends also to emphasize the unexplored and far away, and land where no white lady had been before or which no Englishmen had visited.

THE SETTING

Connie came to the Naga Hills travelling from Calcutta up the Brahmaputra river by steamer as far as Guwahati, then by cart (later railway) to Dimapur in the plains below the hills. Another cart took her climbing up through the forested slopes on the main track to Kohima which continued on to Manipur. To reach other destinations in the Naga Hills District British officials followed footpaths or the government bridle paths, with their bungalows or rest houses every 15 miles or so. The hills are steep, the ravines deep, the going beyond the bridle paths strenuous. To leave Kohima and travel over this land Connie had to walk, ride and sometimes get carried in her 'topper'.

Much cooler than down in the plains, Kohima was a small hill station of the British Raj, where the headquarters of the Naga Hills District was located, a collection of 'mud huts and tin roofs', with barracks, schools, a hospital, the odd shop and bungalows for the few British with their gardens, pets and servants. Close by was the largest of the Angami villages with its 800 houses and 3,000 people. The DC (Deputy Commissioner) was in charge of the district and security was provided by a regular battalion of Gurkha Light Infantry and the Naga Hills Military Police.

A forerunner of today's Assam Rifles, the NHMP was a paramilitary force responsible for policing and protecting the district. LWS, as commandant of the battalion, was required to inspect the various outposts manned by his men and it is on these tours that he took his wife. These were 'inspection visits' – he was not accompanying the DC. Connie's travels took her as far as Henema (Tening today) in the south and Tamlu in the north where small squads of NHMP were located in forts. She also travelled outside the district to Manipur.

With the establishment of the Naga Hills District the British applied their law and administration to villages which had to give up their old customs of raiding, slavery and head-taking, bringing about a pacification. The villages had to pay a house tax and supply labour when required and in return were afforded protection from attacks from outside the district. The British followed a policy of minimal interference when it came to the internal affairs of the village, the administration of which was maintained through Naga customary law under a gaonbura (headman) and a village council of elders. So in this time before Christianity took a hold the old culture in the villages, the social divisions of the khels (clans), the morungs, the material culture, all continued, without the violence. Blood feuds were no longer allowed to run. The Deputy Commissioner adjudicated in cases that village councils were unable to resolve. The people lived off agriculture, hunting in the forest and some limited trade. By 1900 the district was generally peaceful except for occasional warlike incursions from the Trans-Dikhu tribes over the border.

Beyond the river Dikhu lay the 'Unadministered Area' with its 'wild tribes', occasionally visited by British officials with their military police. Between this area beyond the border and the Naga Hills District was a so-called area of 'Political Control', visited but not administered or protected by the British.

Accompanying her husband, Connie, seemingly undaunted, travelled in both the area of political control and in the district, where they would meet the gaonburas and the dobashis (interpreters), effectively intermediaries between the colonial power and the villages. An escort of NHMP 'rifles' always went with them.

Naturally LWS must have been a strong influence on his wife and the way she saw the world around her. He had been in the hills two years before she came and earlier he had seen service in the Lushai hills, another region of the North East. A quick glance through his books will tell you he was a realistic soldier. But while he appreciated and respected the war-fighting approach and abilities of his opponents he believed not in indulgence but in stern justice, in taking strong measures of repression, in punishment and reparations, in 'salutary effects', in the unequivocal threat or decisive use of force as the means of control. Some quotes from his writing will illustrate this: 'Nothing impresses these wild folk more than a surprise show of force', 'These posts among savage tribes are the only means of really controlling them' and 'The present day absurd sentiment of 'making friends' … in a hostile country'. A quote he takes from Major John Butler (written in the early 1850s) clearly appeals to his way of thinking: 'Greater boldness and presumption are always sure to be manifested by savages where their aggressions pass with impunity or their acts of violence are not instantly chastised. On such occasions procrastination or forbearance on our part is construed by them into fear'. His frequent use of words like 'treachery' and 'intrigue' suggest his wariness and distance from the indigenous people. A 1920 review of his *History of Upper Assam* closes with the sentence: 'Although he does not say it, his idea is *Speak gently and carry a big stick*'.

The British first visited the Naga Hills in 1832 when their progress was resolutely opposed. Thereafter they gradually encroached on the independence of the hill villages. Over the next 50 years British policy wavered between disengagement and pushing forward with punitive expeditions, the problem being to keep the hill people from making raids and 'depredations' on the plains and tea gardens of Assam. In 1877 the base of operations was moved up to Kohima from Samaguting on the edge of the plains. The years 1879-80 have been described as marking the end of the military phase of colonial rule although this ignores the Ao region which came under British control only by the end of the 1880s – an area visited by Connie just 10 years later.

The colonial record often made the Nagas responsible for the annexation of territory: 'Depradations and raids necessitated taking over the tribal areas to ensure peace and prosperity as civilisation extends'. The imposition of British authority over the Nagas involved punitive measures, these being the burning and destruction of villages, the confiscation of cattle, the extraction of fines and the imposition of imprisonment in the Andamans for ringleaders of rebellion. To quote one report: 'Burning (a village) has had the usual wholesome effect'.

The colonial writers recording this gradual subjugation were soldiers and administrators who wrote reports, papers and books on the subject. Style varies: they could express dismay at the 'treachery' and the 'depredations' but they could also be clear-headed, objective, and show appreciation of Naga characteristics. Sometimes they took an ethnographic turn and could even be affectionate. They recorded relationship building and occasional mutual respect. But ultimately the relationship was one of power and there was a common underlying attitude about the two contrasting worlds of western civilisation and the primitive world with its 'savages'. Again some quotes from the period will illustrate this: 'Like all wild uncivilised tribes', 'The task of pacifying and humanising these primitive hill people', 'Very low in the scale of civilisation', 'Civilising barbarous savages', 'Natural insolence of savages'. In the year after Connie arrived in Kohima the DC wrote in his general administration report: 'The Assam-Bengal Railway is now open to traffic as far as Nazira, a result which almost brings Kohima within the pale of civilisation'. This underlying British assumption of superiority made for a condescending, patronizing, paternalistic attitude toward the Nagas. This was the imperial mindset.

Connie's liberal use of the word 'savage' and her colonial attitudes come from this background and from her husband. So also does her knowledge of the colonial record and the Anglo-Naga conflict. She was aware of some of this history in the villages she came to know like Kohima, Khonoma, Chadoma and Kekrima. She was also aware of Kuki-Naga rivalries and the assault on Phesama by Johnstone's forces in 1879.

Without a written record it is not so easy to gauge the attitude of Nagas toward the British. Some 20 years earlier Mrs. Cawley, survivor of the siege of Kohima, had written of men from Khonoma who 'had sworn to exterminate the invader'. More than a century later a Khonoma author wrote: 'as soon as the British left their villages after imposing fines and punishments, the villages started to plot again as to how they would strike back at the detested colonizers'. In 1900 the tribal peoples of the North East had not finished with revolt.

In 1917 the Kuki rebellion lasted two years and in the 1930s Jadonang and Rani Gaidiliu led another one in the Naga Hills. In 1900, although the 'wild and barbarous, treacherous and bloodthirsty' Nagas had now been subjugated and pacified by the British and were no longer the recalcitrant indigenous villagers they once had been, the British were not accepted by everyone as part of the landscape.

When Connie arrived in Kohima punitive expeditions were still not a thing of the past. In 1897 LWS had been involved in a cross-border punitive 'promenade', as they called it. After she arrived he took part in another across the Dikhu, in January 1900. This came to be known as the Yachumi incident – an occasion that resulted in serious casualties for the eponymous village. A third punitive raid across the Dikhu followed in the summer of 1901, launched from Tamlu. Besides these expeditions, the NHMP had to intervene after 'serious riots': in 1898 between two khels in Changki resulting in seven deaths; in June 1900 between two villages leaving a number dead, one of the villages being Mao Thana which Connie was to visit later. And in 1902 in Nankam Noel Williamson, a political officer they knew well, was personally involved in a battle between two morungs. In addition to these larger disturbances, crimes such as murder demanded police attention. The Naga Hills were now more peaceful than they had been in the 19th century but this was a peace built on the 'rifles' of the colonial power.

Nigel Shakespear

Chapter 1

Tour to Henema[1] – May 1900

May 1900 –   Trip to Henema the Katcha Naga country.
Our three selves and Col. Molesworth, 44th.

5th Breakfasted with Capt. Woods who gave us a noble "set off" and then started down the cart road, taking our English mail to digest on the way. We hadn't gone 2 miles before down came a pelting shower – that chased off, but only to come on harder than ever a little further on and we finished our 11 miles to Khonoma fairly drenched through. Col. M. has been very seedy so we are anxious he had not got a chill and I fancy he is really none the worse. It's a nice little Bungalow, well built, only a little damp being only lately finished, and has a lovely view of Khonoma village most picturesquely situated on an almost detached looking hill, commanding the whole of the valley into which it juts out, with Mozema on the further side – two of the biggest Angami villages. Hot Tea, fires and a dry change have set us all up.

6th 16½ miles to Paona. Got off about 10 a.m. and breakfasted about 9

---

1. According to Robert Reid the name Henima was an Angami name and its correct name, Tenning, was hardly recognised. The bridle path to the village was made in 1885. (Reid, *History*. 1942).

'Carved gate at Jotsoma' May 1900

miles out in Zulhein valley. A big climbing zigzag up to the top of the hill above Khonoma, and Lel walking all the way as Assimoo had gone lame, and L. had put him up on his pony, B. and I sharing the other. A glorious day and the Forest most lovely, till we came to the more open country of the Zulhein valley. Yesterday's storm must have been heavy here, as there were large drifts of frozen hail lying deep in all the gullies and the Cliffs up above were glittering with ice. The last part of the march was very trying, very hot and very steep; I got into my basket chair on the back of a Naga, and B. and Col. M. rode while Lel walking found it rather a strain, poor fellow, I fear at the end of so long a march. The scenery along the valley is simply lovely, the Zulhein running below, to our left, beyond that Forest covered hills with every variety of foliage in all the freshness of its early Spring tints and blossoms. At the upper end of the valley is Paplongmai, or Kenema, an important village. This is rather a miserable little bungalow, 2 rooms, and mud floors, and all rather tumble down but the situation is lovely on the top of the ridge with magnificent forest all round. The Gadflies are a regular plague!

'Khonoma' May 1900

'Paona Rest House El. 8100' May 1900

7th Monday 16½ miles to Lakoma. Got off about 9 a.m. and breakfasted about 7 miles out on Chama ridge, getting in about 5 p.m. The Bungalow here has been unroofed by the wind in this last storm, so we are putting up in the soldiers' shelters and doing very comfortably, and Col. M. has got his tent. The Gadflies here too are very bad. (An awful storm here all night).

8th 19 miles to Jasoma. Got off about 9 a.m. changed coolies at Berrima[2] 7 miles and breakfasted 2 miles further on. A very hot and long march, which I finished up in my "topper". Such pretty "catstail", mauve orchids on the trees just outside. The Gadflies terrible, and had to be kept at bay by fires of rice.

9th Wednesday 13 miles to <u>Henema</u>.[3] Started about 9 and breakfasted above Sarama, and very hot it was. The last bit of the way was the steepest bit of climb I've ever known, compassed by a path. B. wanted to walk! but was at last prevailed upon to ride when L. and Col. M. did the same, and I got into my "Topper". A lot of men came out to meet us at the bottom of the hill and it was amusing and pleasant to see their curiosity and interest in us.

---

2. Some 60 years earlier the first British official to visit Berrima was Mr. Grange who in 1839 saw the remains of a circular fort built by a Raja of Cachar, a onetime invader of the hills. When the Raja abandoned this fort he left behind a 10-pounder gun which was shown to Grange. A good hint to the British perhaps. After that visit Butler, five years later, described Beereh-Mah villagers as being traders in ornaments, conch shells and beads adding '.. it is said that, till very lately, it was the great mart on these hills for the sale of slaves'. (Mackenzie, *NE Frontier.* 1884: Butler, *Travels and Adventures.* 1855).

3. 'We then had 7 outposts far apart, and which commandants were ordered to visit at least twice a year; they were – Khonoma 50 rifles – Henema 25 – Wokka 25 – Lozema (Sema country S.E. of Wokka) 25 – Mokokchung 100 – Mongsemdi 50 – Tamlu 50. These were permanent, then there were patrol posts at Veraru – Zubzu – Piphima of 6 rifles each to patrol the high road, as robberies from carts were frequent; and almost each year we were called on to locate punitive posts of 25 rifles for several months in offending villages. All these gave opportunity for much touring on the part of the commandant.' (LWS, *Memoir* [written for his son]. 1926).

'Berrima village'

'Rest house and earthwork fort Henema Kacha Naga country'

'Entrance to Henema fort'

'Henema village' May 1900

They had never seen ladies before. Several attached themselves to my Topper to help me up the hill, one carrying, 2 pushing, laughing and joking all the time, putting me down at intervals to take breath and then coming round in front to look at me and see how I was getting on, talking, laughing and smiling at me, apparently enjoying, and finding great fun in the task they had undertaken! The walls of the little Fort at the top of this precipice, more or less, were lined with interested spectators, Nagas and Goorkhas watching our approach, who welcomed us with many salaams and much talk (alas! that we did not understand it!) as we arrived. Such a pretty little Fort it is – earthen bastions, the centre part laid out in a level parade ground bordered on each side with gardens which soldiers interest themselves in keeping up, and all in such perfect spic and span order. Lel took us round the Fort and village, Col. M. much struck with the smart appearance of the place. The air is delightfully cool and invigorating up here, very refreshing after the heat of the march.

'Kacha Naga village of Duphima near Henema'

10th Halted. Did some sketching while Lel was busy at his inspection work. Henema and Duphima villages sent in their troupe of men and girls all in Gala get-up who danced for us all evening, in spite of a very heavy thunderstorm. The dance is very curious. They begin by ranging themselves in a long line, men leading, girls following, and start a slow, harmonious chant, accompanied by slow beats of their drum, and to this they march round slowly, sometimes they divide, and one party intertwines with the other, or counter marches, the speed gradually increasing as also the volume of sound, till at last it becomes a most energetic and noisy performance, but always very pretty – the singing always antiphonal. After the dance round they stop, and certain picked girls come out and dance, form together, a sort of reel dance with different figures. Being so wet we let as many as could come inside the verandah, all very cheery and full of interest in us – the girls very prettily dressed but rather shy.

11th Sketching all morning, and then on the range after breakfast watching a match at volley firing, for Lel's prize of 10/-. Later Junia and Sarama villages sent in their dancing troupes, all eager to dance, but space hardly allowing of the two parties, nevertheless they kept it up, the noise becoming quite deafening as in their increasing excitement they banged their drums harder and harder and shouted louder and louder. While these two parties also were dancing, sounds approaching from the distance told of a third party coming! but it was getting too late then for them to do anything.

'A ballet[4] at Henema by Kaccha men and women' May 1900

12th Off again homewards once more though we would all have liked to stop longer had time allowed. Frightfully hot down at the bottom of the hill, so was glad to ride a bit. Breakfasted ½ way and reached Jasoma about 4 p.m. After tea strolled in the village which is prettily situated. Found it quite cold and were glad of fires and dined indoors.

13th Lakoma. Up at 6 and got off by 8 – a hot march. Breakfast half way and met a party of sepoys who said there had been a slip on the road beyond this – a bad lookout for our baggage ponies.

---

4. 'Dancing is one of the principal amusements in a Kachcha Naga village. There are two kinds. The first is a war dance with spear and shield, in which the men alone take part: and the second a general dance, in which the women share. The latter has many figures, and is danced in pairs, the men and the women facing one another. Music is supplied by the non-dancers, who stand in two rows and keep up a chant which varies with the nature of the dance ….. The dance takes place at night by the light of fires and torches. The women (all unmarried) display their finery and best clothes, and appear most thoroughly to enjoy themselves. (Soppit, *Kachcha Naga. 1885*).

Henema, May 1900

'Principle⁵ dancers' May 1900

5.   Soppit's description of dress does not really match these photos: 'The ordinary male dress is a short kilt of blue cotton cloth, reaching from the waist to halfway down the thigh. Below the knee a number of finely cut pieces of cane, dyed black, are worn occasionally. The upper part of the body is bare, though a large cloth is generally carried for use as a shawl in cold or rainy weather. The ears are ornamented with rings, bright feathers, or flowers, and conch shells are worn around the neck. The women wear a cloth reaching from the waist to the knee, blue or white, and on occasions of dances or festivals a white cloth with coloured borders and triangular patterns of various colours worked in the centre'. (Soppit, *Kachcha Naga. 1885*).

'Street in Henema Kaccha Naga'

Henema, May 1900

14th <u>**Paona**</u>. A very long march, but pretty, and the latter part shady in the forest, which was lucky as it is all up hill. I did a good bit in my "Topper" leaving the ponies to Lel and B. but my men got very slow towards the end. The road had been mended up, where there had been a bad slip, and our ponies came safely over the zigzag this time where, going, one of them had gone over the side falling some distance down, but being loaded with bedding rolls which acted as buffers, fortunately took no harm.

15th It is so lovely here we have halted another day. Lel busy climbing up to Paona peak looking for orchids while B. and I sketched. Never having attempted a forest sketch before I find it very difficult.

16th Khonoma. A most <u>lovely</u> march. Coming through the Zulhein valley again we found all the banks of the river and every little gully down which ran a stream, lined with the most lovely tall, white lilies all come into bloom since we last passed through. Also in the forest we came upon wonderful plants, huge leaves standing as high or higher than Leslie, with marvelous blossoms rising from the root about a foot to 2 ft. high, dark crimson with light spots, something like a huge flycatcher, a deep pocket nearly covered. B. and I dug up some splendid plants of Domusida [?] fern, and other lovely ferns, orchids too, my "Topper" and an empty "jhapa" being filled with our collections.

'Jasoma'

17th Halt at Khonoma. Did sketches of the village and the "snake house" up at the Fort, but both very difficult. The pony went ill, we found him in the stalls immovable as to his hind legs, and using them as a pivot to get round on his fore legs. I gave him all my store of peppermint and ginger in a bucket of warm water – hope it may do him good!

18th Kohima. Those ponies played us false after all, <u>would</u> not get well, in spite of my efforts for their good, and I had to foot it the whole 11 miles in. A bit tired, but none the worse, and after a lie down in the afternoon quite ready to enjoy our dinner up at Capt. Woods.

'Paona'

Chapter 2

Tour to Tamlu
July and August 1900

July 22. 1900. <u>Tesima</u>. A lovely day for marching as soon as we had left behind the fog of the Kohima valley; with a gleaming light, like a spring day at home, bringing the most lovely colouring over the endless ranges of mountains and valleys and what made the likeness still greater was the singing of the birds, the pleasure in it all the greater for its rarity, one bird's song being exactly like that of the dear old home Blackbird. The garden is brilliant with a particularly pretty sort of sunflower, and all aglow generally with balsam etc, magnificent ginger blossoms too, which just now blaze out everywhere like flames amid the jungle. Went out with L. in the evening to look for a bird's nest we knew of but found the birds flown but it was a pretty walk.

23rd Chichama. 7½ miles. Got off about 10.30 and started with 1½ mile of what we thought about the steepest incline possible down a most rocky path, part of it towards the bottom being a stream bed, till we reached the bridge over the "Nerima pana" at the bottom. Here we stopped to breathe and then began the ascent on the further side, no delay occurring in our realizing now our conception of the angle of the former incline was quite mistaken as to its possibilities, for this was infinitely steeper – and oh! the heat! Never have I been so overpoweringly hot, every few hundred yards of such an ascent was quite enough for me. I mounted my "Topper" and therein with short intervals, finished the ascent, but the heat and discomfort still continued great. Well we have had a good experience of a Naga path. Where hills are concerned,

Naga paths go as near perpendicularly up and down them as it is possible to arrive at. It took us 1½ hours to get up this one, after passing Nerima the road improved and we had it very fine and pleasant for riding the rest of the way in here. In the evening we went out to see some very curious graves which are close by, graves surmounted by wooden effigies, cut out of a single block of wood, one figure very complete with arm and neck ornaments carved with it, the other only a head surmounting a plain block on which were carved the representations of no less than 26 heads; evidently the grave of some great warrior, the 26 dummy heads representing the number of live ones he had taken in his day.

24th & 25th Themokadima (Rengma) 13 miles. Such a wet march most of the way, but thank goodness more level than yesterday's. Had it only been fine all the way it would have been most enjoyable, for our path lay all along the mountain side where at first starting the views were glorious, and then later this forest ground full of lovely flowers and ferns. With waterproofs and on the ponies backs B. and I managed to keep dry for some time, but after some miles we got stiff and tired riding at a foot's pace so got down and walked, not exactly good walking as the path was mostly standing water all the way! So that by the time we got in we had not much about us that was dry. However we were none the worse; Leslie administered sips of rum, and after a dry change we sat down with good appetite to a lunch at 3.30, having started 10 a.m. Here we are in the Rengma country having left that of Angamis in our march yesterday. The people do not compare well with the Angamis at all, the latter being fine, well grown and often handsome in appearance and very smart and tasteful in their dress and ornaments. These people are all the reverse, and as to their village which we visited yesterday evening its squalor and dirt was simply appalling. Their houses though are rather picturesque with their gable ends filled up with a sort of semi-circular verandah which is built into and across it. Just opposite to the bungalow here is a large patch of the hillside covered with little miniature huts raised on piles. These are the Dhan houses, or little store houses in which the village keeps all its rice, thus placed outside the village and below it so that in case of fire, to which these villages are very subject, their food supplies would not be destroyed along with the village. A man came hobbling up this morning suffering from Snake bite, just been bitten while at work in his field. "What could we do for him?" The only thing that occurred to me was "Scrubb's Ammonia"! which we promptly dabbed on, Leslie having scarified the place with a big needle. Added to this we gave him a fair amount of raw whisky after which he cheered up and finally one of his friends picked him up on his back and carried him off apparently much better.

– The people here bury their unweaned children in their houses, others all about their village.

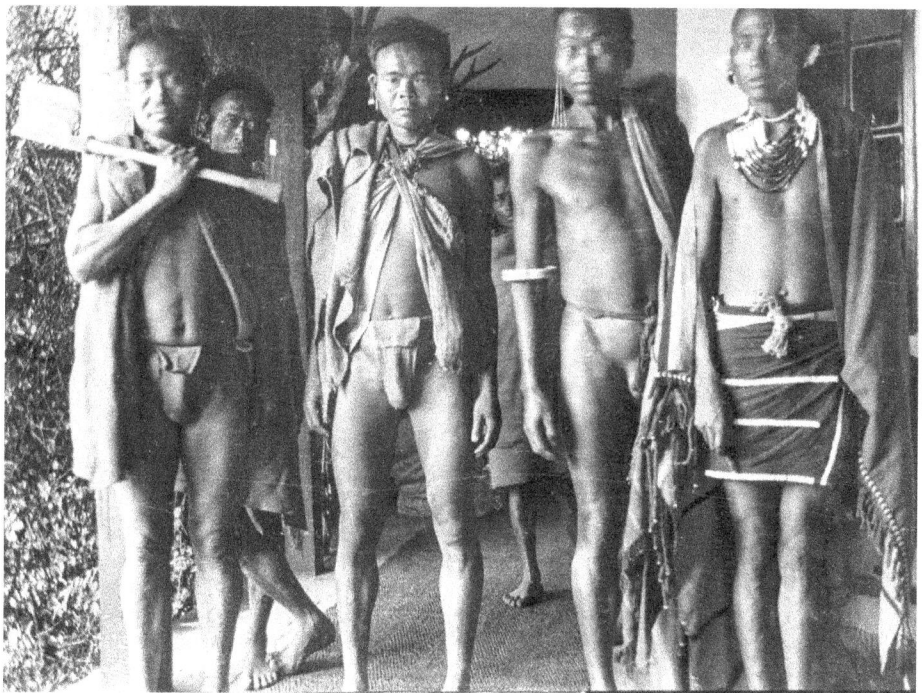

'Pochiris from Melomi'

24th Kotiama 9 miles. A pleasant march, a fairly level road, with a bright sky, sunshine and cloud, giving the loveliest effects of colour, light and shade over the endless ranges of mountains. In this these mountains vary from the Himalayas in that their valleys are all narrow and shallow, more spread out so as to be capable of cultivation and in the whole landscape not one acre of level ground is to be seen. On our way we turned off to see Insima [?] a very pretty looking village and most picturesquely placed on the top of a hill among magnificent trees, but the heat was too great, and only Leslie could face it while B. and I turned back and hurried to get over the last 2½ miles before the gathering storm came up. Leslie overtook us and as we got in photo'ed us both on our studs! a most unique sort of picture I expect it will be! It has been a lovely evening after the storm and from the verandha, with glasses, we can even see the Dunseri as it flows through the Nambhor forest and the hills on the other side of the Brahmaputra, and beyond the Mikia hills are quite plain. Have got a horrid sore throat and feel a worm! the working up of a cold which has been hanging about for days, caught from B. and L, which is hard luck!

27th and 28th <u>Wokka</u> 9 miles. Capital of the Lota Nagas, a very debased, unsightly looking people. E. 5,100ft. Such a pretty little place, once a "station" with a considerable garrison, but now no European officer lives here, and the place is in charge of a native Asst. Commissioner and only a force of 20 N.H.M.P. occupies the Fort. The latter crowns one of the 3 little knolls which are the feature of the place, is very smartly kept inside, beds of flowers filling the spare places, and outside has a deep V shaped ditch and high bank. Our Dak bungalow crowns the other knoll just opposite while on the 3rd knoll and a little further off, is the house now occupied by the native Asst. and the new Post Office which is in course of building, and the picturesque little thatched married quarters for the Sepoys, lying on the lower ridge between these two knolls. Below in the middle is an undulating stretch of smooth turf with fine trees scattered about it, looking much like part of a private English Park, and beyond this is a little Goorkha settlement, thatched cottages with gardens round them, where pensioned sepoys have made their homes. A pretty walk has been cut the whole way round the place, "The Ladies' Mile", and passing along part of it in the evening we saw some of the finest Tree Ferns we have yet come across, such lovely graceful things, and a most wonderful wealth of other beautiful ferns. It was a most pleasant march in, fine weather, very hot at times certainly, but a nice fresh air which helped one along, and we had great fun part of the way over catching butterflies, so gorgeous and so plentiful all the way. Our net is not a good one and our success, B's and mine, was but small; it being difficult to catch anything while marching with no time to stop for anything, but this L. would not believe, so took the net saying <u>he</u> would show us the way! Needless to say his efforts accompanied by our jeers were for a long time no more successful than ours! but at last he caught two beauties, one a rich blue, with pale spots, which I was particularly anxious to get. There were others, scarlet, orange, white and mixed colours and one like a great bird, canary body and brownish wings, which I <u>hope</u> yet with patience to get hold of some day! I have also got some caterpillars, marvelous in size, colour and development which go into empty tin boxes on the way, and which some of them are even obliging enough to have begun cocooning already when they will be less trouble to carry.

29th Koio 8 miles. E. 4000ft. Lhota Naga. A pretty march, the first 2 miles up hill, for the rest mostly downhill, the path winding in and out along the Forest covered mountain side with many pretty corners where the mountain streams come tumbling down making lovely waterfalls embowered in beautiful ferns. The people of these parts smoke a queer shaped pipe with a deep reservoir attached to it for catching the nicotine. This they collect and put in a wide basket-work bottle which they carry in their waist cloth and drink occasionally as a relish. Among the Sema Nagas it is a very delicate compliment when a lady offers you a drink of nicotine from the bowl of her pipe. This is a very pretty, cosy little bungalow, and wonderfully fresh and cool considering its elevation. A wonderful view just above here over these endless ranges, so marvelously blue in their distances, right onto the plains with the Brahamaputra quite plainly visible. Just below this range is the valley of the Doyang which we cross in tomorrow's march. The Doyang is the great river of the district, the boundary between the Lhotas and Rengmas on one side and the Semas on the other; rises near Maothana on the Manipur Road about 20 miles beyond Kohima, and fed by its principal tributaries the Sijoo and Zuloo, with a varied course trending mainly North by West falls eventually into the Dunseri. Two more caterpillars, quite active when we started, had cocooned by the end of the march. A speedy resignation to circumstances, truly!

'Carved tree trunks at Koyo'

30th Lungtyan. 10 miles Sema Naga E. 3000ft. A horrible march, scorching hot though we started at 7.30 a.m. For the first 7 miles the road is a steady descent for 3000ft. down to the Doyang, getting hotter and hotter as one went down some of the re-entrants where no air was moving, being absolutely suffocating. At last we reached the Doyang, a fine big river but at this season very muddy; Leslie and B. took a photo of the bridge and then we started on the ascent of 2000ft. in 3 miles, and if the descent had been bad the ascent was even worse. I bustled on as fast as I could on the pony, got in about 11 and sent it back to help L. up, who came in with B. on the other pony about ½ an hour later, both fairly done. As for me I don't know when I have had a worse "head". I can't stand that furious heat. Happily a heavy storm came up soon after we got in, which was a great relief. This is only a very narrow strip of the Sema Naga country which we pass out of tomorrow. The people are a wretched looking lot as is usual with the Semas of the low hills and much afflicted with the most unsightly wens[?]. About 10 miles from here is the valley of the [*leaves a gap – the Dikku is the river*] the boundary of our Control, beyond that the country is independent and unsurveyed and mostly unknown.

31st Lungtum or Nankam.[1] Aoh Naga. E. 5400. 11 miles. A much pleasanter march, very hot, but all ascending, and the air consequently improving as we went until with some steep zig-zags in the last mile we arrived at this glorious position at the top of a spur from wherever as you sit in the verandah of the Bungalow you see on your left, beyond a few ranges of hills, the Assam valley laid out, with the Brahmaputra stretching through it, the horizon closed in by the pale blue lines of the Himalayas above which in clearer weather may be seen the Snows. A little less than ½ right the line of the valley ceases while immediately in front the hill on the horizon shows where Tamlu is, overlooking the plains, and the final point of our march and from there on to our extreme right is nothing but a sea of mountains, perfectly magnificent, Mongti a notable point, showing up against the sky, the view finally bounded on our extreme right by the Barail Range, and the whole, as now, looking most glorious in its varied effects of sun, cloud and storm. The air is most reviving and as there are some of L's N.H.M.P. here to visit, and there is much to see in the picturesque village which lies below, we are going to stop here over tomorrow;

---

1. In 1887, before Nankam came under their direct administration, the British burnt all the head trophies in the village which later asked for a British post to be stationed there. (Reid, *History*. 1942).

it will be refreshing. I should add that the Dikku running more or less North and South and the boundary here of our territory lies about 7 miles from us on our right, and the mountains beyond that all belong to the Patkoi Range. Part of our road this morning lay through forest and as we came along we remarked what a land of exaggeration this is; the road side ferns were at least, some of them, 10 and 12 ft. high, the common worms on the pathway 12 or 14 ins long, the butterflies, many of them as large as birds, the beetles also to be measured by inches, and so on. Another point we were also remarking on is the unfailing good temper of the people. I have never yet seen any exhibition of bad temper among them, no children quarrelling or fighting, no angry mothers scolding or cuffing their children, nor as I say, any quarrelling at all, nothing but good temper and good will. A little incident struck me yesterday evening. A troop of children under charge of one elderly woman were coming home to the village, their path lying past the Cookhouse where all our servants were collected. The children were laden some of them, with branches of wild figs, their little cloths filled with them too, and as they passed one of our boys catching sight of them ran out and took a branch of these from one of the little lads. No demur was made on his taking it, the little lad gave it up at once and the boy, hot with his long march, began eating them at once greedily. Others seeing him thus enjoying himself wanted some too, so ran out to get more from the other children who were passing and these at once opened their cloths, gave them all they wanted and ran on their way playing and well pleased, and it seemed to me that English children would not have allowed themselves to be thus despoiled of their fruit with such goodwill.

'Corner in Nankum Village, Aoh Nagas, July 1900'

Untitled

'In Nankam village' 1900

'View of Mokokchang'

Aug. 1st <u>Mokokchung</u>.[2] E4,500, a pleasant march, 11 miles, fairly level and at times cloudy, which is always a relief. We left Nankam passing straight through the village in order to get a good view of their "Cemetery" which lies at the end. The "burying" customs of these people are very curious, in fact I should not say "burying" for they do not bury, I should have said <u>funeral</u>. As soon as anyone has died a little enclosed shelter is built onto the front of the house, the dear departed is put on a sort of framework and for from 3 to 5 weeks there he is smoke-dried by fires lit underneath him. When quite dry he is wrapped up in a parcel with leaves etc. and is placed in the "Cemetery" on a little bamboo platform, raised about 10ft. from the ground, the body having a little bamboo matting cover of its own, and the platform being thatched with matting also. Underneath this and about "the parcel" are hung certain of the departed's ornaments, or if too valuable to be left to rot, for instance, the Boar tusk necklaces, which are very valuable and the iron of their Dhaos and spears, iron being also very

---

2.   The British had moved the sub-divisional headquarters from Wokha to Mokokchung ten years earlier, in 1889, owing to increasing raids of the Trans-Dikhu tribes, bringing the territory from Mokokchung to Tamlu under their administration, constructing a bridle path between the two. (Reid, *History.* 1942: Sema, *British Policy*. 1991).

valuable, dummy representations in wood are made and placed in their stead. This Cemetery was most picturesque, a long line of these curious little hutches, of various heights, sizes and ages, stretching down the hill slope and under the shelter of a line of fine trees.

This is a little bit of a place, its central point the Fort which is always picturesque. The principal Bungalow of the place is occupied by the Sub divisional Officer, Mr. Williamson, away on tour just now. There is a tiny "Kutcheri", two so-called "shops" (?) and a few other buildings. There is a garrison of 80 men here, so Leslie has a fair amount of inspection and musketry to do, which will necessitate our staying here some few days.

9th Mongsemdi,[3] 15 miles. E. 4,500. A long march necessitating breakfast on the way which we had very comfortably in a shady corner in the Forest where a beautiful stream crossed under the road. Sibboo had gone on ahead and had got fire lit, the stew hot, and the kettle boiling so there was very little delay in us setting to at the breakfast we so much needed by noon, having had our first light meal about 7 a.m. Then on again after breakfast and it got very hot after leaving the forest, till about 3 miles out 3 sepoys met us with a supply of Tea (?) well sugared and milked! but no matter what it was, it was drink! and as such most acceptable. As we approached here the Sepoys pointed out a valley just below where they told us the elephants were very fond of coming up, and had been quite lately. Here there is a Stockade in place of the usual earthwork Fort, a palisading of Bamboo forming the fortifications, with sharp bamboo spikes, hardened by fire, fixed in the palisade and facing outwards, looking like an exaggerated porcupine's back. We were to have stayed here over tomorrow for Leslie to inspect the Fort but we hear Mr. Williamson S.D.O. from Mokok is coming in so we must move on to make room for him.

---

3. In 1888, following a raid by men from across the Dikhu which resulted in the death of 148 villagers, the British stationed a guard in a stockade at this village. A subsequent attack on the stockade at night was beaten off and the guard remained in what became a permanent post. (Reid, *History*, 1942).

'Mongsemdi stockade Aoh Naga country'

10th Santong (Chantung) 13 miles E. [*gap*] made an early start getting up at 5 a.m. and again taking our breakfast to eat on the way. We did a lot of butterfly catching on the way, getting some very good specimens, but of course missing the finest of those we were most anxious to get. At Susu village we turned off the road to go through the village and were there overtaken by Mr. W. who joined us and came back with us for breakfast. First though we were taken by the Headman of the village to his house to see some cloth he had for sale, but there the atmosphere with the crowding up of the villagers all round us was really a little more than we could stand, so we moved off to what perhaps may answer as the "village club", a cane-work platform covered with a thatch roof and with open sides which was far pleasanter, but even here the crowd did it's best to supply the deficiency of walls! most effectually keeping out the faint breaths of air for which we gasped, and had to be constantly driven back, only to return again and again with much fun and laughter, and endless curiosity. At last the calls of hunger summoned us to seek our breakfast, so Mr. W. and I hurried on leaving L. and B. to take one or two photos and to follow, and at last about noon, and 2 miles further on, we all assembled and discussed a most welcome meal in a pretty shady place by the roadside. But the heat! I don't think we any of us felt hotter, and as for B. and L. they were a sight, and the quantities of fluid we all managed to put away were astonishing. Mr. W. then left us and we came on our way here, glad indeed to get in at last after such a

'A village orator - Santong village (Aoh)' 1900

hot march. It is a wonderfully picturesque village, the view of the end on which we look from the verandah being a perfect picture in itself. The long lines of houses are built with wonderful regularity all along the top side of the hill, as is the fashion of all the villages in these parts, the effect being very striking indeed, with a few fine trees here and there varying the lines. A tremendous storm came up in the evening, with magnificent effect on the mountains, and thunder such as made one jump, but the coolness was a great relief.

'LWS and Noel Williamson[4] at Tamlu'

'Santong', log drum[5] 1900

4. Williamson, killed in the Abor country in 1911 which prompted a military expedition north of the Brahmaputra, was described by John Shakespear [a cousin of LWS] as 'one of the best frontier officers who had a charm that enabled him to make friends with the most surly strangers'. (LWS, *Memoir.* 1926: Shakespear, *Lushai Reminiscences.* 1929).

5. Possibly one of 'Nagaland's most ancient log drums' from 1725 or 1740. (Van Ham and Saul, *Expedition Naga*, 2008).

11th Merongkong, 8 miles. E. 3,100. Such an interesting start we made going through Santong village, accompanied by all the society of the place, led by the Headman, Monti, a pleasant mannered very fine looking fellow. Having arrived at the further end of the village, nothing would do but we must honour his house by going in to drink some of his Zu (rice beer) so in we went through the entrance portion which is common apparently to cows and pigs which are herded here at night, on into the living room where are their cooking, eating and drinking utensils, their few cloths, and the matting where they apparently sleep, all very dark, having no outlet but the door at each end, but well ventilated through the floor and the sides. Here Monti with some dignity as host and head of the house, drew up his red cloth, a sign of honour,[6] which they cherish, spread it on the bamboo mat and sat down, drawing his 3 children about him, leaving us to look round his mansion and the chung or balcony at the back, while his wife, a pleasant looking woman with many necklaces, and in a dark blue cloth, the raiment of the village, busily washed out 3 bamboo mugs, filled them with Zu and presented them to us to drink. All the time a smiling and deeply interested crowd which had followed us in stood and watched and laughed and chattered, while Mrs. Monti having completed her hospitable effort sat down also beaming at us and pointing out her children to us. Having drunk what zu we could we moved on, having exchanged signs of goodwill with our friendly entertainers and such few words suitable to the occasion as were common to our mutual understanding, a very limited few but at the door were stopped by another old man, the "Goan bura" of the village, wearing the Government red cloth in honour of his position of Revenue collector, who begged us also to honour his house! It was a little trying, as time was getting on and the sun getting hotter, but in we had to go, getting off quicker though this time as we could not drink more Zu. At the end of the village we came on a curious sight, a case being tried by the local village powers. The "Judge" was a fine old fellow who standing up was haranguing the "Court", (lines of men seated opposite him on the opposite bank of the street) and pointing each period of his speech by a violent dig of the spear he held in his hand into the mud in the middle of the street. There was tremendous emphasis in this. I am afraid the solemnity of the business was a little upset by our arrival, and the attention of the "court" somewhat distracted, its members all turning round to gaze at us, and breaking into broad grins when they saw our

---

6. The British gave a red cloth to gaonburas to wear as a badge of honour.

intention of photographing the scene, yet the old "Judge" went on haranguing and prodding quite undisturbed only so far relaxing as once to break into a grin himself for a moment.

'Merankong village from above' 1900

'Corner in Merangkong, Aoh village, showing how the houses are supported' 1900

Untitled

The march in was easily got over being so short with a long descent of 4 miles, with a rise again of 3 miles. There were wonderful ferns along the way, lovely corners where masses of these feathery things, 12 or 15 feet long and broad in proportion, made most exquisite effects. Also we came across many traces of elephants, footprints, and the curious tunneling which they make in the long "elephant grass" sometimes 20ft. high, pushing their way through it up the hillsides towards the crops which attract them higher up. We took a walk in the village in the evening, the usual admiring crowd hovering around us. It is a big village, built in 2 long lines chiefly, along the crest of the hill, the ground nothing but bare sloping rock which made it marvelous how any building could find grip in it. Two curious beings appeared to pay their respects to us, from two friendly villages in the independent country. Jaetong, Headman from the village of that name, and another man a "chief minister" from Bortablung, who having eloped with one of the Rajah's ladies, has now got to live this side of the border if he wishes to keep his head on. This latter is decorated with an elaborate necklace and earrings, which in his own entourage constitute his whole attire, but in deference to us he has hung a silk cloth about himself. Jaetong who is a nice looking fellow has had his whole appearance ruined by some misguided missionary having presented him with a huge and ancient "pothat" and a black coat to correspond, both of which he was constantly believing them a great distinction as showing his intimacy with the Great Power. Such a shame to have turned so fine a fellow into such a guy.

12th Tamlu. E 3,000 Lengta Naga A stockade, as at Mongsemdi, and a garrison of 25 N.H.M.P. Only an 8 mile march which we got over nice and early. A very pretty road, part of it with frequent traces of elephants along it; one tree had only just been freshly broken across the path. The little Stockade which adjoins the Dak Bungalow, has a very fine situation on the end of a spur from whence there is a grand view all round, over the final range of hills and the Assam plains which here come up quite close, only 5 or 6 miles distant, while on the other side the Dikku runs immediately below in a deep valley beyond which is the Independent country, a boundless sea of hills. It is curious to think how one has arrived now at the furthest limits of civilization and that only so short a distance divides us from a country utterly unknown and unexplored and peopled by absolute savages whose one pride and delight is to find an opportunity or excuse for fighting, murdering and cutting off heads. One man who was showing us through the village at Meronkong the other day, as we

'Tamlu stockade'

passed his house, pointed out to us five skulls hung up in his verandah which he claimed with the greatest pride and a beaming face as his own personal sport, and added how much he should enjoy taking some more only our rule had forbidden it. These Lengtas[7] also as a rule wear no clothes at all, none whatever, as signified by their name which means "naked", the only things they wear are ornaments, necklaces, earrings, a belt made of stained bark which they draw in very tight round them, making their bodies bulge out above and below in a curious way which suggests much discomfort but does not seem to incommode them, with a small flat lying tail of the same hanging down from it behind, and quaint caps made of bear or monkey fur covering a

---

7.   Connie's description differs somewhat from that in the *Census* of 1891: ' In physique they are superior to.. (the Aos), while in dress, general appearance, cut of hair, and language they are entirely different. The dress of the men consists of a few strips of blackened rattan cane or a broad strip of white bark bound tightly round the waist, a large tail of bark being often left hanging down behind. Add to this garters of cowries or strips of cane dyed red and armlets of the same with, on great occasions, a helmet and a few stripes of white paint on the face, and the costume of a Tamlu brave is complete'. This goes on to say the men are tattooed on their chests (heads depicted) – Connie makes no mention of such nor do her photos show this. (Davis, *Census*. 1891).

framework of cane, with boar or pig tushes fastened in patterns all over them. The Trans Dikku people wear conical caps of bright coloured very fine woven grass. Their funeral rites are smoke drying, after which the body is put in a boat shaped box and hung up in a tree, while the head, having been broken off is put in an earthen jar or wicker basket, and placed at the foot of the tree. The Trans Dikku people hollow out lumps of sand stone[8] to hold the heads.

CMS footnote: To cut off the head would seem an unfriendly act that being their final act of vengeance on their enemies. It is therefore broken off and received in a cloth by the widow (in the case of a husband's death) who stands at the head of the ……

13th Tamlu. We have been down to the village trying to sketch a very fine and highly ornamented Moranghur, but find it a most difficult subject, dependent on so much detail. The Moranghur answers to a bachelors' club where all the unmarried men live and each village has two or three. The Semas, Angamis and Cacha Nagas do not have them in a pronounced form, any unused house is appropriated for the purpose, but among the Aohs, Lengtas and Trans Dikku people very fine, imposing buildings are erected especially for the purpose, and are much decorated. In the evening while at dinner the "minister" and "his court lady" from Bor Tablung with a very curious and striking looking friend came and joined us, sitting on the steps of the verandah while we finished our meal, they discussing rum (diluted) and cheroots the while, also some sweet biscuits which they rather approved. The lady, a plump sturdy, good humoured looking little body was loaded with necklaces and earrings, a most picturesque object of barbaric finery, and wore a little petticoat of very fine weaving, distinctive of Bor Tablung, and the desire of L.'s heart; if he could only induce the wearer to sell it. A deal for it was begun, the husband taking the opportunity to assure us then how in this romantic elopement they had left "all" behind, and had no possessions now but such as they stood up in, a case of "the world well lost!" and an argument towards a better price! Nothing final was arrived at then, and L. dropped a rupee into the lady's extended palm, as she rose up to go, and the court couple departed, taking the cookhouse on their way, to see what further they could get there to supply the wants which love had left so unsatisfied!

---

8. Badgley's report on burial customs of villages around Tablung is similar: 'The head is invariably removed after death. It is twisted off after decomposition has sufficiently advanced (to cut it off would be a supreme insult to both the dead and living relatives)… placed in a cylindrical vase of stone..' (Badgley, *Surveys Report*. 1875)

'Tamlu. Moranghur' August 1900

14th Tamlu. Such a changeable climate. The day we arrived so hot that we could hardly bear our clothes and hunted about for the coolest corner outside where to put our dinner table – then yesterday a storm and quite fresh and cool, today oppressive beyond words, but again this evening after a storm almost cold in the wind. This morning we went to sketch another still more picturesque Moranghur than yesterday's, but it was a bad day with me and nothing would come right. Since then we have had a most amusing conversatzione, our friends the "court couple", Impi (the lady) and Ayoh, having come up to see us and arrange about the petticoat, being weather bound here by a heavy storm and therefore on our hands to be entertained and amused the while. Impi stood near the door till her husband made us understand he would like to see her seated on a chair, when we brought another up and she came and seated herself on it alongside of me where I was sitting writing at the table. Very pleased and satisfied was her husband seeing her thus seated alongside and just like the lady! and very funny did she look, for never before surely had she sat on a chair and she did not know at all what to do with her fat little legs which dangled down below and could not reach the ground comfortably. Then the bargain for the "petticoat" was concluded and she got up, took it off and wrapped it around me with much laughter and clapping of hands in admiration of the effect.

'Io/Ayo and Impi', Tamlu August 1900

The entertaining of our company was a little difficult as no verbal intercourse whatever was possible between us and the lady and the two friends who sat outside the door, and only a very few words, helped out with signs, could be exchanged with the husband. but a cheroot was produced and handed to the lady which she smoked with much satisfaction for a while and then passed on to her husband, then I handed them my hand mirror and that was very amusing, the way they looked at themselves, handing it round from one to another, then I brought out my sewing materials and showed how they were used and that interested them and Leslie brought out some finished sketches in pen and ink of the Moranghurs here, which they recognized at once and discussed most intelligently, to our great surprise pointing out the various details – a degree of comprehension one would not have expected of such savages. And then finally B. and I got our Mandolins and Guitar and that was a great success, never could we have a more appreciative audience, "A Franquesa" set our "court minister" dancing, while the lady nodded marking the time all through. We played several pieces all evidently giving much pleasure, but had to resort to "A Franquesa" again as finale to produce again the stirring effect with which we had started. The music over, Rum (and water) was produced for our guests, when Ayoh seeing the bottle of Zu which he brought as a present yesterday, pointed to it and said we must drink too, so we toasted the lady who quite understood the little custom and laughed, raising her cup and nodding to us in return. On the whole they were so entertained that it was a little difficult to get rid of them even when the rain had well stopped, but at last it was accomplished but only after I had been persuaded to present Impi with one of my coloured muslin shirts!

15th Merongkong, once more and I feel quite sorry that our backs are turned on Tamlu, which has for so long been the objective of our daily march. Our start was very funny. Leslie having some reports to hear was delayed so B. and I started ahead our friend Ayo accompanying us, and doing his best to make us understand how much regret our departure caused him. After going a little distance he seemed to think that some final attention on his part must be shown us to express in some way if possible the depth of his feelings towards us, so turning to B. he took her by the hand and so escorted her some little distance down the hill. Well, as everyone knows, anything more than a little of this hand clasping becomes a little disconcerting and B. began to wonder how long it would last, and how she might end it without offence to the gentleman while I walking behind had full enjoyment of the little scene. The gentleman however knew quite well what he was about and when he thought B. had had enough attention shown her, he dropped her hand and took mine, and so escorted me along, giving my hand little gentle pressures and talking the while and making signs which I gathered meant that his heart and mine were one! Most affecting. We thought it quite a scene not to be lost so B. halted us while she took our photo, thus hand in hand, to the gentleman's supreme satisfaction and then in return I made them hold hands and took them. One dared not laugh for fear of hurting the gentleman's feelings, difficult though it was not to do so, but there was a still greater trial to come, for on starting again he took a hand of each of us so we two were both conducted with much dignity and state down the hill, the while his converse became still more emphatic than ever, and we thought it was quite as well that Impi, his Bride, was not there to see us. He now proceeded to give us to understand that the hearts of all three of us were one, and it is my idea from the impassioned style of his speech and pantomime that he sort of proposed to both of us! It was getting more and more disconcerting and ludicrous when a little halt occurred and we took the opportunity to break up, and offered him the "English Salaam" of a handshake and thought that that was "Goodbye"! but no, he took the handshake and seemed half inclined to stop, but on second thoughts again took our

'Trans-Dikku Nagas at Merankong. Group of Lengta[9] Naga' 1900

hands and conducted us a little further. Then it occurred to me that the Farewell must come from us, so I stopped and we again said "Goodbye" as far as we could, and this time he loosed our hands, and with a face expression of unutterable regret he waved us away with an action of hands and head which seemed to say "Go, words are of no avail, alas! Farewell." It was <u>all</u> expressed! and we continued our way alone while he turned back. If only we could have had L. to photo us, the <u>three</u> walking hand in hand! such a very funny sight it must have been! – It is a pretty march but was very hot, so I got on the pony shortly and pressed on as fast as possible so as to send it back and pick up L. for the last 2 or 3 miles if possible. This evening we went for a walk through the village up to the further end, accompanied of course by a crowd as well as by "Molong" the Goanbura who conducted us. It is curious how among these ab-

---

9. In this photograph the men wear aprons as they do in all diary photographs taken in and around Tamlu. This contradicts Connie's entry two days earlier that 'these Lengtas also as a rule wear no clothes at all, none whatever, as signified by their name which means "naked". Were these aprons donned for the photography?

solute savages their manners are instinctively pervaded by little courtesies and attentions. The streets are very rocky and steep, in some places almost precipitous with only little notches cut for footholds. Coming down these our friend Molong hovered round B. and me, holding up our dress behind us in turn so that it should not get soiled by the steep rocky bank, also, afraid that I might slip holding my arm to support me and so helping me down, to say nothing, at the steepest place, of putting his arm round my waist to make quite sure of me! He took us into his house also and did the honours of it making us drink some of his Zu. In the evening after we got home and as it got dark all the invalids of the village came up, introduced by another Headman, all expecting to be treated but of course our means, travelling thus, are very limited, such as cough mixture, sirup and remedies for Dysentery which seems now rather prevalent, and ointment for cuts and wounds. For a poor consumptive girl we could do little beyond giving her something to ease her cough and itch and it was touching to see her there the first thing next morning before our start with two fresh eggs as a little offering of gratitude.

16th Santong. (Chantung) A very hot march indeed, but I got over it quickly, as before, sending the pony back for L. In the afternoon we started out, I with a pony as I was feeling tired, to visit the village of Louan about 1½ mile distant most picturesquely situated on the top of a wooded spur which sloping on one side, on the other goes sheer down 2,000ft into the Dikku. It was very pretty and very interesting, more especially as I don't suppose any European womankind[10] had ever been near the place before, but the heat was appalling, the air being perfectly still and breathless under the hot sun, with that oppression which precedes a storm, which rather spoiled my enjoyment.

17th Mongsemdi. A relief after the heat of the last few days to get into this higher, and fresh, cool air.

10.	Mary Mead Clark, wife of Reverend E.W. Clark, had lived not so far away in the village of Molung since the 1870s and had visited Merangkong. Her husband had visited Tamlu in 1881 with men from Merangkong. Mrs. Rivenberg and her husband had also lived temporarily in Molung in the early 1880s. So CMS was not the first 'white woman' to have been in the area. Similar thoughts can be found in the 1946 diary of Mildred Archer as she muses near Kikruma that 'very few Englishwomen can have passed along this road'. (Clark, *Corner*. 1907: Archer, *Journey*. 1947).

18ᵗʰ Mokokchung. A pleasant march. breakfast ½ way in the Forest, collecting flowers on the way, lovely Begonias, Orchids, Licopodiums etc. Met a most picturesque man on the way, Goanbura of Longsa, the big Aoh village (the only one) across the Dikku. got up in all his smartest finery. so he had to be stopped, placed in the sun and photo'd in front by B. and behind by L.

'Mongsemdi stockade' August 1900

19ᵗʰ Wrote letters, and dined with Mr. Willliamson and Mr. Kennedy.[11]

20ᵗʰ Wrote more letters! And the above dined with us.

21ˢᵗ L. had a competition with ball ammunition for four squads of his men on the Range, which B. and I with Mr. Kennedy went to see. The men never having had anything of the sort to do before were not very quick at picking it

---

11.   Lieutenant W.M. Kennedy was the Officiating Deputy Commissioner and in his Tour Diary for that July he notes 'Captain Shakespear and party have come on here on their way back from Tamlu'. No direct mention of the ladies. Later in 1923, now a retired colonel, he was working as travelling superintendent for the 'Tea Districts Labour Association' when he was found murdered in a train out of Calcutta. (LWS, *Memoir.* 1926: Kennedy, *Tour Diary.* 1900: Reuters, *The Register, Adelaide.* 1923).

up and had needed endless explanation from L. to get any idea of it. However they seemed to enter into it at last and did it very well on the whole, but being a dull afternoon light failed before the 4th squad could do it. As it was Mr. K's birthday we dined with him and Mr. Williamson, being entertained with his excellent Champagne which he had ordered up for the occasion. Lel and I gave him a Mozenjami poker work chunga as a little souvenir.

22nd L. very sorry for himself after the dining out, but off early to put his 4th Squad through their competition while we packed up for start. Such beautiful butter to be got here that I collected 5lbs washed and salted it and put it down in a biscuit box to carry away. Such butter is a treat, and what we took away from Mokok in the same way was delicious up to the last of its 17 days. We did not get off before 12.30 going up to the Fort first where I presented the two first successful squads with their prizes of money, then down to the road where we overtook Mr. K. who walked the first 5 miles with us. Nankam was made about 4, a good deal of rain on the way. Tumsi as usual hovering around and Bindong with her hospitable offering of chillies and cucumbers. Alum Khaber, the chowkidar, such a bright and smiling fellow with Bhootas, and all Tumsi's brotherhood in fact. L. and I went for a turn in the village in the evening. It is a very large village with 2 or 3 streets. The one we went down had a tree in the middle of it in which in former days it was customary to hang the trophy heads brought home from warfare etc. All that it bore now was a few ancient Ghurrahs as a sort of souvenir of its former honours. The houses are built in 3 degrees of state – the plain ones with simple overhanging gable ends for the common herd; a sort of semi-circular verandah roof built into the gable end signifies that the occupant is the owner of many pigs and the gable raised high and filled up with a high pointed piece of thatching, after the style of a Moranghur signifies the possession of cattle and Mitton and that the owner is a man of some importance. There are also small houses built especially for the unmarried girls who live together in them apart from their families. The Bamboo matting which forms the front of these houses was particularly well made here, with a pretty pattern woven into it. I don't think I have said anything of the endless uses to which the Bamboo is applied in these hills. It supplies every implement almost of domestic use. Water is always carried in lengths of the large Bamboo, you often see a load of these filled with water stacked in a basket being carried from the spring to the village and our bath was always filled here from a monumental pipe of this sort, adorned all

'Headmen at Masungjami'

'Corner in the Aoh Naga village of Nankam Miss Ingram taking a photo' August 1900

its length with rough patterns of snakes. The cups, drinking and eating vessels are all lengths of Bamboo, longer, shorter or wider. Their pipe bowls also are pieces of Bamboo and we ourselves have to employ bamboo now for egg cups and it answers admirably. Their houses of course are all Bamboo, poles and matting, and often bamboo leaves for thatch.

23rd Lungtyan. A grey day more or less and therefore pleasant for marching and we got in comfortably about 1 p.m. Then the sun came out and we got a lot of butterflies the little flower garden being full of them when we arrived. Fairly hot here being so low, but such a fresh wind got up in the evening that I was quite glad to put on a warm coat for dinner, and sit indoors afterwards.

24th Koio. Made an early start alone at 6.10 a.m. getting down to the Doyang bridge by 7, but even then finding it hot enough. How I had to whack that pony to get him along, his thoughts and desires were all with his pals left behind to whom he was always doing his best to return, turning round and trying to start back, and even with his head in the right direction, it was all I could do to get him along. And this was the more provoking as I was anxious to get in and send him back to help L. up the weary 7 miles ascent from the Doyang. Got in at last about ¼ to 9, and was glad to find that L. got him about 3 miles

'Luntiang rest house El 4000' '

out from here, he and B. not arriving till 2½ hours after me. Two Goanburas came down to meet L. and bring him some Zu, and there was much laughter over their compliments to him to the effect that he was indeed a very big man to have two wives! and that the ladies were pleasant to look upon! They can't understand that B. is not his wife as well as me!

In the evening we went for a stroll in the village, on the hill top a few 100 yds. from the bungalow. Such a pretty, picturesque village, and so wonderfully clean, and well swept looking, though sweeping is a thing they never do. The village too was at its prettiest with the bright sunset light on it, and the busy life in it which is only found when all the working community come back from their days work in the fields. As we made our way down to the further end of the village we came upon such a pretty little social scene, a party of men and boys, resting on their return from work, some of the older men with their babies on their knees, while the women for whom they had been working, and in front of whose little house they were gathered, passed round from one to another handing them food from a large kaf, sometimes into leaves which they held, but as often as not straight into their mouths. A nice young fellow who could speak a little Hindustani joined us and as it were did the honours of the place for us. He was the son of the old Goanbura who had died a few days before. He pointed out the grave to us placed just in front of his house, in the street, covered over with green boughs and with 4 bamboo posts at the corners with sort of little basket work sconces on the top of each, and in each of which wrapped in a plantain leaf was a gourd of Zu, as refreshment for the departed, while a fire, which he told us would be kept up for 3 days was burning at the head.

25th Wokka. Such a hot morning for our start – the sun out and the air still and laden with moisture. We stopped at Koio and went up into the village where L. took a photo and by that time were all in a melting condition. However I managed to walk 5½ miles out of the 9 which was not so bad considering the temperature. Hardly had we got in when that dear old man Subedar Major Arjun, who is on leave here and has brought his family out for change of air after the sickly season it has been in Kohima, came up to the Bungalow bringing a most beautiful collection of butterflies which he had made for me since we passed through before, some quite magnificent in size and colour, and among them 2 "dead leaf" butterflies which are rare.

26th Halted at Wokka, and went out in the morning with old Arjun and our butterfly nets to see what we could catch. A most interesting old man is Arjun to go out with, he understands all the habits and ways of all the animals that are to be found in the forest and jungle, from large game to birds, butterflies and caterpillars and can tell you all about them. Also he told us how Wokka peak is mentioned in the "Meru Sagai", and was named after the daughter of a Hindu Rajah of Tezpur in days long gone by and that there was a shrine to Mahadev and Khali in olden days on top of the hill, besides the one which the Gurkhas discovered as still existing at the bottom of the hill when they came, not so many years ago. The shrine at the top of the hill has been lost sight of, overgrown by jungle, but the one at the bottom has been taken care of, a little temple has been built over it, and it is a most picturesque little object standing beside the stream with its group of tall bamboo poles and little many coloured pennons set up by various devotees. We caught a fair number of butterflies but the best were not out as there was very little sun and the afternoon was wet and stormy.

28th Temakadima. (Rengma) A most oppressive day, no sun to speak of, but no air either, the clouds low, and the atmosphere <u>hot</u> and full of moisture. Still we got along very comfortably – it is a pretty march, and out of the 9 miles I managed 7 on foot. Guason the smiling Goanbura was at the entrance to the village with his bottle of Zu for our refreshment. Disappointed in getting no light for taking a photo of Guason and "Johnnie" which we much wished for.

29th Nerima. Started off with a fine morning, the breakfast jhapa packed for breakfast on the way, it being a 17 mile one, and a supply of water included so that we might stop anywhere as appetite or pleasure suggested, without being dependent on finding a stream. Poor Massadi, the Khit, was again feeble and had to be put up on a pony leaving one only for B. and self to ride in turns,

'Con and Miss Ingram at Kotsoma'

and was told to go 8 miles and there halt with the breakfast, leave the pony there and go on. Meantime we walked. It was a beautiful morning, though hot of course, and the road was good and with breakfast and a halt before us we pegged away, doing our usual 3 miles an hour, which for these hill roads is very fair going to keep up. We found a lovely Ginger, different to any we had found yet, a fine head of large blossoms of dark cream, and got up 2 or 3 roots of it to add to our collection, the Flower jhapa being always in attendance now for additions to our stock of plants. Then it began to seem like breakfast time and the inner being to call aloud for sustenance, but still no signs of Sibboo and food were to be seen, and still we trudged on, hoping that each turn of the road would bring the welcome sight in view. But as hope deferred maketh the heart sick, so experience has shown that breakfast deferred maketh something else sick, and at last coming upon a stores jhapa which from its own due weight was fortunately lagging behind the line of coolies, we halted it and with Miltu, the Naga assistant khit to help, we hastily pulled out its contents, finding bread and butter and Bologna sausage and thereon fell to at once by the roadside and did excellently well. Shouting presently elicited the whereabouts of Sibboo who then came up with the customary stew pot, all hot too, as he had settled down about ½ a mile further on, by the 10th mile stone, and alongside of a thick muddy pool, which was his idea of the necessary water! so on the whole we did better than usual, but only just in time, for before we could scramble everything back into the jhapas down came the rain in sheets, and so continued till we got in. We are evidently getting back into the rainy district, and leaving the drier hill ranges behind. A poor little bungalow this – under a hill and not much view.

30th Tesima.[12] Back again in civilization more or less, and it is nice to see the dear little garden looking so bright, so much more of the banks and surroundings turfed too, which is a great improvement, and to get into the little house again which is so homelike after the many strange bungalows we have been in. The march was a trying one of course, though short, down the 2.600 ft. in blazing sun to the river and then up the 1.500 again to this spot, all as straight down and up again as Nagas can make it.

31st Kohima. Home once more and dear old "Morning" wild with delight at getting us back, and the little monkey full of demonstrative welcome – had not forgotten us a bit, as we half thought he might have done. The little house has been white-washed while we have been away and looks very fresh and clean and it is pleasant to feel settled again for a bit, most enjoyable though our tour has been. There is lots to do in settling things and drying and cleaning all our belongings which have been left to themselves so long, for the damp has been terrible.

---

12. Tesima was a 'musketry camp' 7 miles out from Kohima where, before the arrival of Connie, LWS had built a 'pleasant little three-roomed bungalow' and would take a company for 10 days musketry. (LWS, *Memoir.* 1926).

'Deputy Commissioner's house and garden' Kohima

Chapter 3

Journey to Manipur
September 1900

Sept. 1ˢᵗ A Baby Hooluk was brought by some Nagas, which at last they agreed to sell for a reasonable amount. Such a dear little creature, all arms and legs and eyes, a fragile little being which seems to have been starved during its long journey from Henema. Very confiding and not a bit wild.

2ⁿᵈ Quite an anxious day with our new Baby, the difficulty being to know what to feed it with and then to get it to eat at all, as it seemed too weak to do so. I got up at 6, and sent Japali out to get some plantains at sight of which its little eyes brightened but it could not do more than nibble at a tiny scrap, and was too weak to move, just lying on one's lap or wherever it was put down so as soon as the new milk came we gave it a little brandy in milk and water and that revived it so that it could eat a little and so with periodical doses it got through the day, eating more and finally getting quite chirpy. We dined with Mr. Kennedy, heard Mr. Pritchard's Gramophone, and came home to find the Baby peering out of its little box, mouth open, with a very satisfactory appetite for more plantain.

4ᵗʰ Leslie went to Kohoma, to see about the garden there, and returned.

5ᵗʰ His Birthday [*his 40ᵗʰ*]. The lamp I got for him arrived in good time and will be ready.

'Japoli our Naga malli in rain hat and grass cloak. (Phesama village)'

7th Leslie off to Tesima.

9th Joined Leslie at Tesima and had 4 nice days out there, very enjoyable, the place so pretty, the views lovely, the air so fresh, and such numbers of flowers everywhere. We took some pretty walks all about the place where I had not been before, one day collecting a quantity of that pretty ground orchid Arundini Bambusifolia which is just now in blossom. Poor old "Bumble" got taken with a fit one afternoon from over running himself and had to be carried nearly all the way home by Leslie, no light work, seeing his size and weight, but the dear old dog was so grateful for the kindness it was quite touching. The little Hooluk came out with me, is a dear little thing, no trouble, and getting very fond of its belongings. We did a lot of developing and printing but without much success unfortunately. (The Hooluck's mark!) [*a couple of lines with smudged ink - Ed.*]

'Squads volley firing Tesima Range 500 yds'

13th Returned to Kohima to pack up for Manipur.

16th Made our start for Manipur – breakfasted with Mr. Kennedy and then started our cart, and ourselves followed later about 3.30 with the traps Col. Maxwell and Mr. Hodson had sent up for us from Manipur, Leslie walking the first mile with us. We made Jakoma, first stop, about 6 p.m. ahead of our cart, no lights, but managed Tea from our baskets and the cart followed about 7 p.m. No Sibboo (cook) and only poor feeble Massadi to get dinner ready and serve it too.

17th Mao [1] – cloudy, wet and almost cold. Kapani the Headman, with whom we made such friends during our visit in July greeted us with smiles and welcomes and a lot of our lesser friends here have come up too to greet us. Such friendly cheery folk it is pleasant to see them again. Still no Sibboo and only poor old Massadi to the fore, who nevertheless manages very well. The little Hooluk is the centre of much attraction among all the small fry who constantly come up with small offerings of wild fruit etc. for it. In return they get a bit of bread and jam sometimes which they like much. This is just inside the Manipur district, as shown by a Guard of Manipur M. P. posted here.

18th Mao. Finished off a sketch from the verandah, but the paper had gone bad so it was not satisfactory. Had a very pretty walk in the evening up on some pretty grassy slopes full of flowers, and cut some Gungaru sticks which we burnt and peeled sitting over the fire in the evening, for it was really cold, the place being 1000ft. higher than Kohima and the evening fresh and windy.

---

1. In June [1900] LWS was out at the Tesima musketry camp with Connie and Miss Ingram when news came of a serious riot between the villages of Khuzama (in the Naga Hills District) and Mao Thana in Manipur. He rode in to Kohima that evening, and 'picking up 25 rifles marched at night for Khuzama 19 miles off and at dawn visited both villages'. His memoir continues: 'Between them 18 (I think it was) had been killed and many wounded who were sent in to Kohima hospital. A wire had been sent to Imphal and after placing posts in each village and arranging to patrol the neighbourhood I went down to Kairong and met Hodson who was bringing up some of his M.P. Together at Mao we went into the trouble (forget what it was) located punitive posts in each village for six months and the trouble quieted down'. LWS first wrote his memoir at least 15 years later and details slipped – as Kennedy's *Admin Report* for the year shows: '… a collision between the village of Mao in Manipur and the village of Khuzama in this district. The quarrel arose over the division of a deer killed in the chase, and next day Mao appeared in force before Khuzama, it is alleged, in consequence of a challenge. A fight occurred, in which the Khuzama men used spears. Four men of Mao were killed, and a good many on each side wounded'. (LWS, *Memoir.* 1926: Kennedy, *Admin Report 1901'*.

'Genna stones at Maram'

19th Maram. Started the cart off about ¼ to 9 with all the servants, ourselves staying behind for breakfast which we arranged for ourselves with our Tea baskets. Then the tumtum was brought up and packed and we made our start soon after 11 a.m. A very pleasant, breezy morning, but getting warmer as we went, of course, as our way was all down hill. It was a comfort to find that the bits of raw, uncrushed metalling which wearied us so all the way to Mao, ceased there; the Manipur Raj not caring for metalled roads. Still there was enough to keep one well occupied as driver, to get over the road at all decently full as it generally was of stones, rocks and nuts. Thirteen miles of this sort of driving rather palls upon one yet the scenery is very pretty. This bungalow stands on a ridge of open grassy downs, and is very fresh and breezy, with a lovely view each way.

20th Maram. An easy day spent mostly in the verandah, a lovely air and not much sun. A very pretty walk in the evening over the grassy downs which we found full of orchids, the beautiful white "Elephant ear" and the "Arundina" and a very fine pure white Ginger. The little Hooluk provides us with much amusement, is developing a conscience which sends it into hysterics almost when it is found out doing what it knows it should not, and is very funny when reproved for reaching out towards the food at table, buries its face in its hands and pretends it wasn't doing anything! It is the dearest, most cuddlesome little creature, is never happy away from us, and follows one everywhere.

21st Kairong. Such a sweet pretty Bungalow – might be an English house, stone built, tile roof, bow windows, walls tinted pale green and purdahs throughout of dark red cloth – quite luxurious. The river nearby is crossed by ford and by a bridge and has excellent fishing in it. Leslie joined us at Maram taking us quite by surprise appearing on his bicycle on which he had come all the way from Kohima in 2 days. He tried some fishing in the evening but had no luck.

22nd Kangpokpi. 13 miles. On the banks of the Tiki river, a nice cool bungalow of the Mao and Maram style. L. went out fishing in the afternoon, B. along with him, while I having home letters to write was to join them later. Inu Ram, the orderly, duly came back therefore to lead me to where they were, and pointing out the direction, after we had followed the road some little distance, we plunged into the tall grass to make our way down to the river's edge. The grass was far over our heads and the ground rough and full of holes and Ino fought his way in front while I stumbled along in his wake. At last we got through and shouted and coo'eed but all to no account. No answer came, so after waiting some time, as it was getting dark, there was nothing for it but to turn round and plough our way back again through the grass. We had not been home 10 minutes before L. and B. turned up, soaked to their middles – they had lost their way when it got dark and so had had to walk back along the bed of the stream. Such a pretty garden here – lovely roses, tube roses and quantities of violets, also a capital vegetable garden.

23rd Kanglatumbi. 12½ miles. A very pretty march indeed following the Tiki river all the way. At one point we photo'd a lovely reach of it, of which we got a good view from the corner of the road, the river tumbling and rushing along over its rocky bed, with high Forest covered bank, along which the road ran, on one side, and on the other, the open valley ground with all the lovely colouring of reeds and water loving plants. This bungalow is just the same as the last except that it has some nightmare like paintings and mouldings over the top of the centre room cupboard. After we had settled ourselves in to our dismay we saw another man arriving; this turned out to be Mr. Langhorn the subordinate P.W.D. officer from Manipur, come out to meet and fetch in Mr. Pritchard who was coming from Kohima also for the Pujas. B. and I therefore had to double up together while he and L. shared the other bedroom. On the way we pulled up at a little group of huts, Sengmai, the spot where in the rising of 1891 Mr. Melville of the Telegraphs, and Mr. O'Brien a Signaller,

'The Tikki river - Kaithenmanbi'

were murdered by the Nagas of a neighbouring village. There was a halting place and small hut here in which these two, ignorant of there being anything amiss, were having their dinner, when suddenly the Nagas, incited thereto by the Manipuris, fell on them killing O'Brien on the spot, but only wounding Melville who escaped into a little stream nearby where he lay hid. He poor fellow was unfortunately lame so could not get very far away, and the next morning the Nagas followed him up and killed him. They are buried close to the spot in a little enclosure and with a headstone relating the event, which L. photographed.

24th Monday. Manipur. Such a pretty drive, all the first part; and indeed all the rest too, though not pretty in itself, is lovely in the view of the opening out of the Manipur valley, the unfolding of the hills enclosing it, and the nearer approach to all the features of this most beautiful bit of country. Pretty wooded hills rising from the middle of the plain were pointed out to us as islands in the big Longtak lake, a wonderful resort for all sorts of water fowl shooting and a never failing rich preserve for the small English society of Manipur. Other smaller lakes and jheels there are excellent also for fishing and for snipe and duck..

– To the right of the valley as you get a little further in rises the "summer resort" of Manipur, Kanjubcul, a hill.. 000ft. above the valley where there is a comfortable bungalow, at the disposal of the Resident, and where in the hottest months the ladies of the place, if any, are glad to get a little change.

'Graves of Melville and O'Brien cut up by Nagas in /91 Mayonkong'

Manipur lies to the left of the valley as you enter it, our road winding round many spurs, all trending left (East) wards. Mr. Langdon kindly lent us one of his ponies to go half way, our own being therefore sent on ahead, so we got along gaily. Arrived at .... where we were to change ponies we discovered Mr. Hodson[2] (Asst. to the Resident) our host who had come out to meet us, and who rode along with us till within 3 miles of our destination when he made us change into a trap which he had waiting for us there. The getting in was a difficulty which had to be done by signal and then the animal, after standing up on end, proceeded to bolt, as I thought, but it proved to be his normal behaviour and Mr. H. knew what he was about. – The curious thing about Manipur is that there is no native town or city. It strikes you as you come in and still more does it strike you when in the evening you see the enormous, crowded outdoor market which collects daily about 6p.m., thousands of women selling wares of every description, the women doing the business, and the men idling about. Where do they come from and where do they melt to? for one sees nothing of their dwellings. Well, we got in safely, the Bagleys (3rd

B.I) coming out on the way to greet us and found a most English-like house, beautifully furnished, put at our disposal, Mr. H. having turned out of it, to occupy the old one in the same compound, which had been his till the State built this palatial new one. The kind little man is doing us royally and we find a programme of "events" which stretches over the next fortnight.

'Doorga Pooja fete' Manipur, September 1900

2. LWS first met 'old Tom Hodson' (Thomas Callan Hodson) in July 1898 while touring to Mokokchung, arriving at the Wokha resthouse at the same time 'from opposite directions in a terrific storm and drenched through'. Hodson was later transferred to Manipur and went on to publish 'The Meitheis' in 1908 and 'The Naga Tribes of Manipur' in 1911. Elsewhere in his memoir LWS relates: '… a visit was paid to Togwema where I saw and photographed the very remarkable Stonehenge, since then only visited by Hodson and Hutton. It was on this visit of Hodson who was on tour disarming Manipuri villages that his trouble took place. A Naga carrying a stack of old muskets bolted down the hillside with them and Hodson fired dropping him. Unfortunately the man died of the wound, and as there were one or two other rather summary actions of Hodson's which Government did not approve of he was outed'. *[The details of this incident differ across sources. Ed.]* Following a military career in the First World War Hodson became the first William Wyse Professor of Social Anthropology at the University of Cambridge. (LWS, *Memoir*. 1926: *Wikipedia*).

'Our sitting room' Kohima, 1900

Chapter 4

To Khonoma
October 1900

14th and succeeding days, life goes on in its quiet round of work, tennis, walks and occasional "dinners" out and at home – only on 16th my birthday was kept, marked by a "dinner". Capt. Woods, Mr. Kennedy, Mr. Grant and Mr. Humphries (44th) and dear old L.'s present was a most dainty little Manipur necklace, gold and the sacred "tulsi seed" in memory also of my most providential escape from a very serious accident,[1] a thing for me to remember with <u>much</u> thankfulness; and from dear old Tom, and Lil a dozen pretty pocket handkerchiefs of lovely Madras work.

22nd We are in great grief today over our dear little "Morning's" death – dear, <u>dear</u> little dog, the sweetest, brightest most loving little creature that ever lived, so <u>human</u>, and so perfectly companionable. Poor Lel, it is hard on him, she

---

1. 'That winter 1900-01 was spent quietly with some touring, and in September we paid a visit to Imphal (marching with carts was the only way then) and put up with Tom Hodson in his new house by the iron bridge over the river. It was during this visit when returning from a shoot on the Waittiok Lake with Tom that your dear mother had a very nasty accident. We were getting into his tonga at Lilang to drive back when the pair of ponies plunged forward knocking her down, a wheel of the heavy tonga going over both thighs high up hurting and bruising her body very badly. We got villagers to make a bamboo litter on which she was carefully carried the 6 miles into Imphal, Tom having driven on ahead to get a doctor out. Most fortunately no serious damage was done, but she was laid up for days and had to lie in the cart the whole way back to Kohima'. (LWS, *Memoir.* 1926).

has for so long been his only companion, and they were so devoted to one another. She was only taken ill on Sat: and this morning between 4 and 5 a.m. she died in spite of all we could do for her. How we shall miss her! and her pretty ways, and especially, I think, the loving greeting and transports of delight with which she always met us when we had been parted if only for a few hours. Dear little thing she will never be forgotten.

23rd Started for Khonoma, B. going on ahead, we two waiting for the pony, and overtaking her about 5 miles out. About 1½ miles further on we sat down in a lovely valley for our lunch facing a most glorious view up a valley with high precipitous mountains on each side, a vista of blue shadows and yellow lights and in front a sheet of golden crop showing up in brilliant contrast. A little stream ran beside us and cooled the milk for us which needed it after its journey in the sun. Our Camp pot was soon warmed up by Japali on a road-side fire, quickly lighted, and we made an excellent meal, followed by smokes by the other two while I tried a sketch of the view before us. Then off again by 3 p.m. and in Khonoma a little before five – a lovely march in perfect weather. It is much colder here, and warm clothes and a fire are most welcome. Khonoma is one of the M.P. outposts, and is most picturesquely situated on a knoll projecting out into the valley which it commands, the Fort crowning the knoll, the village being built all round and below it.

'Near Khonoma'

It first came into notice in 1879 when making a grievance of the small amount of impressed coolie labour required from the village in consequence of our establishment at Kohima it rose, first killing Mr. Damant the D.C. with most of his escort, who had come out to visit the village and then being joined by some of the Khels of Jotsama and of Kohima village, attacking and besieging the garrison under British officers in Kohima Fort. This siege continued for a fortnight and was then relieved by Col. Johnson from Manipur with 2,000 Manipuri troops. An incident of this occasion which is not much known is that the latter on his march up from Manipur was fired on while passing Tessima[2] village, in return for which on his way back Col. Johnson, by way of punishment, let loose his Kuki irregulars upon them who simply wiped out the village; and it was not known till afterwards that it was not Tessima people, but Khonoma people in hiding there who had done the firing, and therefore this terrible punishment was quite undeserved.

– The Kukis are aliens from this country, but are slowly pushing their way northwards, much against the will of all the Nagas of these hills, who fear them greatly on account of their exceedingly bloodthirsty nature. The Angamis are the only tribe who so far have kept them out of their district: they will not admit any within their borders at any price. This however, is a digression. To go back to the "Khonoma rising", after the relief of Kohima the Nagas retired, and in preparation for the pursuit they expected, they withdrew into some fastnesses on the hill above Khonoma known now as the Chukka Forts and there entrenched themselves behind ditches filled with "panjis" and in hollows in the ground whence they could see without being seen, while the sides of the hill were sufficiently precipitous to prevent any enemy approaching them that

---

2. Accounts of this incident vary – Connie is referring in fact to Phesama village and Johnstone describes the incident in his 1896 book '*My Experiences in Manipur and the Naga Hills*' as follows: 'I heard from spies that our Manipuri post at Phesama was about to be attacked by the people of the village, who held nightly converse with emissaries from Khonoma. I therefore determined to punish Phesama.... I sent a party of Manipuri and Kukis who destroyed the village in a night attack, and killed a large number of people. They brought in twenty-one women and children as prisoners whom the Manipuris had saved from the Kukis, who would have spared neither age nor sex had they gone alone'. LWS in his *History of the Assam Rifles* gives a slightly different account: 'Hearing that Phesama village had attacked one of his convoys he despatched a strong detachment of Manipuri and Kuki troops, who surprised and destroyed Phesama, killing over 200 Nagas'. (Johnstone, *My Experiences*. 1896: Shakespear, *Assam Rifles*. 1929).

way. Their women and children they had sent up into further and higher parts of this hill, and thus safe from surprise or attack they remained there watching our futile attempts to get the better of them, from Oct. '79 to March '80, and in that interval by way of showing their independence and unconcern took the opportunity of making their way over the hills and raiding the next big village, Paplongmai, or Kenema, 15 miles off, the chief village of the Katcha Nagas, and carrying off some 200 heads. At last, tired of their comparative confinement and perhaps fearing for their crops which they could not attend to, they came down at the end of their 6 months, and resigned all opposition. The punishment meted out to them was that their ground was taken from them, they were not allowed to settle here again, but were scattered in groups all about the valley where they could find bits of ground to settle on.

'Khonoma "Club", November 1900

None of the villages round would help them, for fear of being implicated in their trouble, and a large Fort with a garrison of 200 men was established on the crown of the hill on which their village stands, now represented by the present small Fort with its section of Military Police. At the end of 4 or 5 years the Khonoma people were allowed to return to their village and ground,

'Look out post - Khonoma Fort'

it being represented that the punishment of banishment from them was too heavy, but it has been much doubted since whether it was a wise policy which sanctioned their return. Though perfectly kindly and peaceably inclined towards us now, they are a very independent and overbearing lot, and a very little would make them lose their heads again.

'Magazine in Khonoma fort'

24th Spent the day sketching the Khonoma hill from the verandah of the bungalow, and the "Snake house" up in the Fort, a most picturesque little Guardhouse on the wall of the Fort and inhabited by tradition by a large black snake, hence its name, but the Snake has not been seen now for many years. Leslie spent his day doing a big climb with some of his men and came back in the evening laden with orchids, 2 or 3 new sorts, other curious plants, and bunches of fruit very like small grapes.

25th Had a most delightful morning out, making our way up to the "Chukka forts" before mentioned, 1500ft. up above this. It is a good stiff climb, so as I have not quite recovered my walking legs since my accident I had a "topper" and was hoisted on the back of a Naga at intervals to help me up. In this way I rather scored, as facing backwards I got a most glorious view always before me over all the surrounding hills, Wokka point rising in the distance, and still further off the distant line of Himalayas beyond the Brahmaputra.

'Khonoma fort north corner entrance. 'Kahoo' 9200' of the Barail Range in the distance'

Arrived at the top it was most interesting to trace out the earthworks and positions of the Nagas, and one understood how absolutely impregnable from below their position was, and could imagine how they must have chortled to themselves, as they looked down on us, watching all our movements which were in full view, and seeing how utterly impossible it was for us to do anything against them. All their older men and women and children were already up there when the first opposition was made to Mr. Damant's approach and they must have watched and clearly seen the whole of that event. We sat down on the raised edge of one of the hollows in which the men had hidden themselves and watched and lived through this time, while our coolies proceeded to cut down all the obstructing branches which interfered with the view till we had a most splendid clear view all round, lighting a big fire also to let their friends below know by the smoke where we had got to. Then down again which was a much easier business than coming up. The hill side is all aglow with a most lovely flowering shrub, clusters of long rather waxy looking standing up blossoms of apple-blossom shade. Quite beautiful. We have ordered some bushes to be brought in to Kohima later on when the bloom is over.

Chapter 5

Tour to Kekrima and Mao Thana
December 1900

Zuloo Valley. 23.12.00. 2.700ft – Made our start this morning for our Xmas week tour, getting off about 10 a.m. It was a funny start, for in spite of all the care taken in preparations to have everything absolutely ready, no sooner had the train of coolies got well under way than it was discovered that various necessaries had been left behind, forgotten, viz the hind-quarter of mutton! the ducks (for our Xmas dinner!), the potatoes, and all these had to be sent flying off by various messengers to overtake the line and get stowed away somewhere among the various loads. I expect the domestics had been having a bit of a carouse over night to account for such terrible muddle and headaches in the morning. At last we got off taking "Bubby" and "Kalu" with us, and leaving behind the Mirrie, the Cat and the poor little Bundu-long; as usual, screaming his little soul out after as we went. We looked in at the Tolleys on our way to wish them "Happy Xmas" and then our march began, a very easy one, good road and all down hill, 10 miles. The orders had been "breakfast half-way" but on and on we went with no sign of breakfast anywhere – the muddle was still thick in the servants' heads and we got into camp at last famishing, to find them there, at 2 p.m., with no attempt at any preparations for food set going!

'Graves at Kekrima - nearer view of graves' 1900

'Terraced cultivation'

Well, a bit of a storm seemed to clear their brains at last, and presently we sat down to a good meal which made new beings of us, clearing out to the last grain the Pigeon Pie which had been destined for our dinner too! We wanted it badly! – Our camping ground is a very pretty one, a small strip of level ground, covered with tall grass, which the sepoys set about clearing away at once for our tents, with the Zulu river running close by, the valley fairly narrow just here with the mountains rising steep each side. Our Camp is very pretty,

B.'s and our tents on either side of the road, Col. Molesworth a little down near the bridge, and our Dining tent between, and in front of it as night fell, a glorious fire of wood round which it was pleasant to sit, and hear the rush of the river nearby and the other sounds of the night as silence at last settled down on our somewhat large retinue.

24th Kekrima. 5,100ft. Such a pretty morning looking out of my tent about 7 a.m. the tall clusters of jungle grass among which we were camped, standing out against the lovely soft grey blue of the distance of mountains and valley. We got off about 9.30, and began rising at once for the 2½ miles over the spur dividing us from the valley of the Siju, and then what a descent! about 1800ft. as straight down as Nagas only know how to trace a path! and so hot, brushing our way through the grass which stretched across the path and over our heads sometimes, holding all the heat from the sun. We were a party of damp, exhausted beings by the time we reached the bottom, thankful to sit down in the shade by the riverside (The Tizu) and to see the preparations for welcome refreshment going on all right and up to time today!

'Con being carried across the Sijoo River, between Kezuma and Kekrima'

'Our camp in Kekrima village', December 1900

About an hour's halt and then from a level of 2.400ft. we began our perpendicular ascent to this! What a climb! I stuck to it as long as I could but had to take to my "Topper" chair, heaved on the back of a Naga, at intervals, and so negotiated the rest of the way, leaving the pony for B.. It seemed endless, but at last we got to a stretch of fairly level path along the hillside and then how lovely the view was, the character of the hillside too, so different to what one usually sees, covered with pines, stretches of smooth grass showing up in such rich contrast of colouring against their dark stems and vivid green. A little further on we came to some level fields on the crest of the ridge, the scene of the greatest fight with the Nagas which has ever occurred, when Blake, in 1854, brought a detachment from Vincent's force at Khonoma and attacked this village, as punishment for raiding etc. It is the only occasion on which the Nagas have been known to come out in force and resist an attack. Seeing Blake arrive with artillery they came out and told him to put those things away and come on and fight it out like men without them, but this of course could not be agreed to and then the Kekrima people swarmed down on them and of course there was a great slaughter, our side also losing heavily. At last after a final steep ascent we got in about 4 p.m. and found our tents pitched in a clearing in the middle of the village, and the kitchen located in one of the houses adjoining, and tea which was quickly brought was most welcome.

'View in Kekrima village when we sketched E. Angamis' December 1900

'Warriors graves shield representation of heads taken by the departed' December 1900

We found ourselves of course the centre of deepest interest to a large crowd of curious and admiring Nagas of all sorts of ages. Such a picturesque crowd and so courteous and well behaved as later on they gathered round and shared the comfort of the big wood fire which was built up in front of our dining tent. Many of them were eating, a large Mitton's horn full of Zu in their one hand, and a little wooden cup full of some variety of grain, cooked in different ways hanging onto their little finger. Seeing we were curious as to their food they handed us samples of it to try, but I can't say we found it very palatable, very hard and very dry. Then it occurred to them to sing to us, so various names were called, their owners coming quickly up out of the darkness; and then after a little consultation the group collected on one side and a more weird and curious performance I never heard.

'View in Kekrima village E. Angami' December 1900

The singers divided themselves into two parties, each consisting of 3 men and a boy, and each group standing with their heads together, the boy in the middle, they sang antiphonally, the men keeping to two deep notes sung under their breath, while the boy did a subdued quavering and somewhat nasal little flourish as solo to their accompaniment also under his breath and this they went on with unlimitedly, with a gentle vibrating effect which seemed almost to mesmerize the listeners, the sort of sounds to mesmerize one to sleep, so subdued and gently vibrating. This is the style of singing peculiar to these people, each clan or tribe having its own distinctive method. It was most interesting sitting there among these queer and friendly people, who had seldom seen any Europeans and never any ladies before, and watching their intense curiosity. Dinner of course was a climax of interest which they watched with fascination.

'Building (repairing) a house in Kekrima' December 1900

25th Xmas Day, we still halted at Kekrima. I think Lel is pleased with his binoculars and I hope he'll get much enjoyment out of them among his beloved mountains which he never tires of gazing over. We took them out and tried them, and they do seem very good ones, then took some photos and after breakfast did some sketching but it got cloudy and very cold and the wind drove us back to Tea and a walk to warm ourselves. It is the season for repairs now evidently and their way of carrying them out is to pull down the roof leaving all the furniture inside the house and then build up again over it all. It was a queer sort of Xmas day. B. and I had to try and make some note of it, so in the interval of darkness before dinner we executed all the Carols we could think of, couldn't think of anything better. The evening set in cold, cloudy and windy and there was no comfort around the fire so we were glad to turn in early.

26th Naukrama. Have had a lovely march and a most perfect day to do it in, very little sun and a fresh cold air. We made our start about 10, and began by a long ascent of about 1000ft. – such a pretty route. It might all have been woodland scenery in England, open grassy hillsides, no jungle, and trees bright with their faded foliage, or else bare of leaves and showing their beautiful, grey lichen-covered limbs. We stopped at Tekabama for breakfast, from whence several parties of boys and lads had come out to meet us on the way, their bright clothes and ornaments making such an effective feature the view. Some of them too as they followed us in long lines along the narrow path sang that pretty chant which is peculiar to these people when thus moving about these hillsides, or coming home from work etc and we could not help stopping to remark how wonderfully pretty it all was. At the village of course we were surrounded at once by crowds and we ate our breakfast, spread for us on a wide seat in front of one of their houses, in front of a crowd some 6 deep, all ranging themselves in tiers, the front row, children sitting, the next kneeling and so on, so that no one need miss "the show"! The road was unusually rough and stony, and I was often very glad of my basket chair. My two men were very funny over it; they said I was very heavy, and grunted deeply and one of them, when it came to his turn to walk behind while the other carried me, made use of my legs as sort of reins by which to guide and assist the progress of his friend who was carrying me, and when I bade them stop, pulled up by them quite forgetting that they weren't part of the equipage, and so very nearly pulled me out! The pony's performance too was very funny – how he managed to get over some of the places is a marvel, but one place was worse than all down a steep slanting wall of big boulders with a stream at the bottom. It was hard for us to get down, and he poor thing having got partly down stumbled and fell, landing on his nose in the stream; but he took it most phlegmatically and finding his nose so well placed remained in that position making the most of his opportunity for getting a good drink! – Coming up to this village, perched on a steep knoll, all the walls and look-out places were crowded with folk on the watch for us. Our tents are perched on different levels, little terraces, in the middle of the village, and of course are surrounded at once by crowds of curious Nagas. The people were very friendly and while we sat round the fire tried their best to get up some intercourse with us chatting and laughing and making signs and, what was unusual, one woman was as friendly as the men and not a bit shy, so that we got on better.

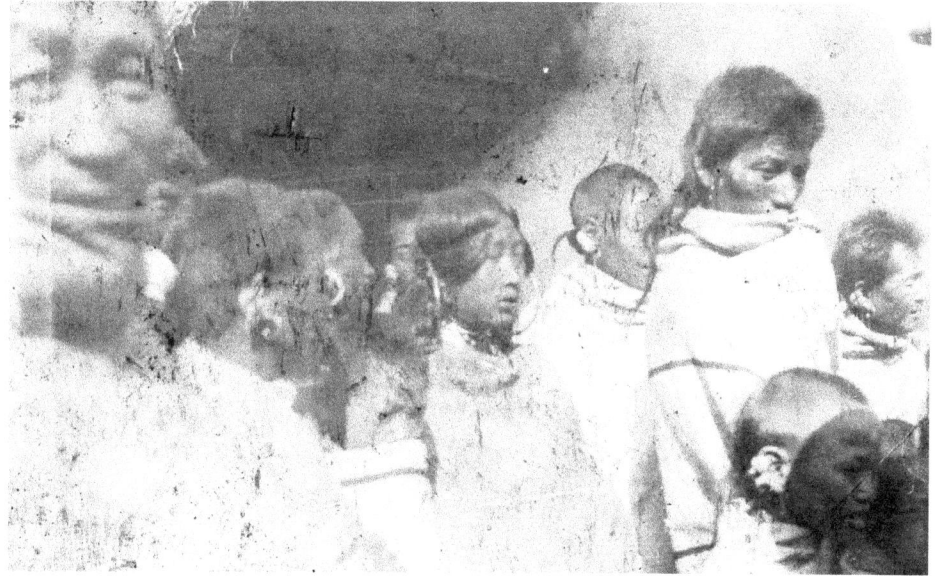

'Tekobarma E.Angami Village belle' December 1900

They were deeply interested in my watch and clothes generally, fingering them and comparing them with their own – took my slipper off and handed it round, and then felt my foot, astonished to find it so soft, their own feet being of much the same texture as an elephant's.

'Narkuma' December 1900

27th Kezakenoma. 9 miles. Another fresh day and the [*air?*] like champagne coming over these heights. We passed by Caloma and then came to Nisami where we halted and took some photos of the houses, then on by Zefizumi to Cherama where we had sent on our breakfast to be got ready for us. Here we were in great luck for we found the village "en fete" dhan pounding and sifting, such a pretty sight as we came down on it from above.

'Nisami Kezami Nagas' December 1900

There were rows of men all in their smartest clothes and ornaments standing on the long wooden troughs with holes in it in which the rice is placed, pounding with thick heavy poles to beat the husk off in time to a most musical chant which they sang all the time. A most busy scene it was, for as fast as the rice was pounded the women and girls came and fetched it, carrying it off to the further side of the "place" where all the girls were assembled doing the winnowing by tossing the rice in basket-work trays, the husks being blown off by the wind. Contrary to usual all these girls were most friendly and jolly with us, not a bit shy, and enjoyed our going about among them – so clean too and nice-looking. I took one of their baskets and sifted a bit which amused them hugely, then one spied my coloured glasses stuck in my belt and I took them out and put them on which elicited roars of laughter, much increased when I popped them onto one of their own noses!

Tour to Kekrima and Mao Thana – December 1900 | 111

'Nisami Kezami Nagas' December 1900

'Carved wooden front and pipes for village water supply. Cherama. Kezami Nagas' December 1900

My watch too was much marveled at, and they laughed immensely over my chatter to and notice of their babies, dear little things in a cloth on their backs. – Breakfast was most comfortably laid on a wide seat in front of one of their houses and of course as usual was quite "a show". After breakfast a deputation was sent up through the interpretation of the Dobasha, to say that the people of this village had never seen a lady or a horse and both being now present they would like to see them <u>together!</u> so I duly mounted, and they all hastened to get the best places on raised "look-out" structures stones and walls etc. so as to miss nothing and I proceeded to give them an equestrian performance (man's saddle) trotting up and down before them. Then they said they'd like to

'Cherama' December 1900

see me go <u>fast</u>! and speed not being my steed's strongest point I accepted Colonel Molesworth's offer of a "persuasive", that is to say he caught him a sound one behind with his stick as I passed, with such good effect that we achieved quite a respectable gallop to the intense satisfaction of the audience who greeted it with unanimous applause! I was quite sorry to say goodbye to such cheery friendly people but we were only ½ way and had to finish our march. The road was rough but feasible for about 2 miles but then came a bit, a descent into a ravine and across a stream which our guide said the pony <u>could</u> not do and we had many doubts too, but we had not gauged his powers, and being relieved of saddle and bridle he slipped down the 200 ft. of almost precipitous drop like a cat and without a stumble, to our great relief of mind.

'Cherama Dhan pounding festival Kezami Nagas' December 1900

Then up the other side, and as we approached this village we passed some of the biggest Ghenna stones by the roadsides that any of us had ever seen. Kezakenoma holds a very high position among all the villages of this district; many of the Angami Nagas and Lotas trace their origin to it and the legend goes that all these tribes are descended from a sacred stone, a huge upstanding mass in the middle of the village, held in much veneration on this account.

Especial good fortune is said to attend this village on account of its possession of this stone, the richness of its yearly crops being ascribed to it. After Tea Lel and I went for a turn in the village and were taken by our guide to see a feast that was going on, rows and rows of people sitting in the firelight, with big bonfires in front of them drinking and eating and enjoying themselves hugely. They were delighted at our coming and honouring them, made us most welcome; we had to drink the inevitable Zu, but were not invited to sample the meat, pork and fowl passed round in chunks in big basket trays, and which the other guests were tearing and rending with teeth and hands! Then back to dinner in our little tent, and the usual gathering round the big fire outside finished the day.

'On path between Kezakenoma and Mao Thana'

28th Mao Thana. We were up early and I managed to get a "snap" of our camp before starting. A long and very pretty stretch of downhill to a river where we halted, and the coolies refreshed themselves and then a very steep climb up, which I did partly in my basket chair. We passed some very quaint stretches of road, the ascent all marked out with Ghenna stones, single, and in groups,

'View on road from Kezakanoma to Mao' December 1900

which we tried to photo but the day was cloudy and I doubt their coming out. A few miles short of Mao having got over the worst climbs we halted in a sheltered spot, for the wind was cold, and had breakfast which was very welcome, then on again, with another very pretty dip with large Ghenna stones scattered about and which we also photo'd. Just inside the Mao gateway I met my friend Ahtika who greeted us warmly, and we took another photo of more Ghenna stones, then on to Kapani's house which we photo'd in all its beauty of decoration and in to our well known quarters here by 3 p.m.

'Genna stones at Mao Thana' December 1900

'Kapani's house at Mao Thana' December 1900

'On road from Jakoma to Kohima' December 1900

29th A very pleasant march to Jakoma with breakfast on the way, and Col. Molesworth more friendly and chatty, and like other people than I have known him all the time. It is bitterly cold here and we are glad of fires in all our rooms, Col. M. however being in his tent, not caring to use the 3rd room here. Found our English mail with letters from Toosie, Lil, Aunt Char, Aunt Mada, – a very jolly budget.

30th Another pleasant and easy march in to Kohima, very cold indeed at starting. Leslie delighted with his Binoculars with which we could look into the fort and see the sentries here from the 1st corner this side of Jakoma, about 6 miles distance. Got in about 3 p.m. and after settling down went over to Tea with Mr. Kennedy, and later on dined there. Mr. Ward came in "thirsting for Leslie's blood" over the Xmas Card of "Mentioned in Despatches" which I had sent him, but which being addressed officially by Lel had completely taken him in on first opening it! and so ends a most delightful tour – everything as pleasant and enjoyable as could be, from 60 to 70 miles in all, of which I have walked about half, I suppose.

'Kapani,[1] headman of Mao' December 1900

31st A busy day indoors and then dinner at Capt. Woods, where we all sat over the fire and sang songs etc. till midnight when we sang the old year out with hands across to "Auld Lang Syne".

1.　　Earlier in 1900, on 24th July, Kennedy mentions Kapani in his tour report. This was shortly after the conflict with Khuzama: 'At Mao I was met by the Jemadar of the Manipuri State Police, and Kepani, the Mao dobasha, who made himself most agreeable as usual, and gave me the names of 4 men in my district who have unlicensed guns. Kepani says all is quiet now between Sopvoma and Khuzama, and that the former bears no malice. I am afraid this is rather sanguine. The Sopvoma people would not be Nagas if they did not chafe under being worsted by a small village like Khuzama'. (Kennedy, *Tour Diary*. 1900).

Chapter 6

Tour to Mokokchung via Ghuckia's village
January 1901

[1901] Jan: 1st Early Parade and 'feu de joie', at which <u>we</u> were all rather sleepy after our late night but the men as usual <u>excellent</u>. In the afternoon sports for the 44th and Police which went off very well and at the end of which I was asked to give away the <u>prizes</u>. I wished I knew more Hindustani to be able to make some nice little speeches instead of the lame attempts which was all I could manage but the men got their prizes! and no doubt that was all they cared about! Dear old Arjun was winner of the Goorkha Officers' race. It was bitterly cold in spite of coats and furs, and B. and I were glad to get back to our fireside.

2nd Busy clearing up and sorting papers with the move home in view. Developed photos in the evening.

3rd Tea and Tennis at the Club. Lel and I actually beating Mr. Ward and B. game to 2. Quite a gathering later with Capt. Somerset, DAAG, Mr. Nightingale C.E, Mr. Knight and Mr. Pritchard.

4th More clearing and mail letters. Developed photos with Lel under great difficulties then a very cheery dinner and evening with Capt. Somerset, Mr. Kennedy and Mr. Grant as guests, and later on Mr. Ward. The band also played for us a capital selection very well played.

'Mithun and group at Ghuckia's' January 1901

5th and following days passed in their usual routine of Tennis and Tea at the Club every other day, letter writing, photography, a little finishing up of sketches and more packing so as to get ahead with it before our next tour and not leave too much to do afterwards.

9th We made our start on our march through the Sema, Political Control country – first of all, before starting, a lot of wires to Cook and Watson about passages, and to Tom at Patiala who suggests my going to him instead of going home. It would be delightful, but I think a few months at home may perhaps be desirable seeing I have lost weight so much, and there's Wyn's Public School to be settled. If one could only divide oneself up into 2 or 3 separate personalities! Well, we got off about 11.30 and made our way down to the 44th Mess where Colonel Molesworth entertained us with a most excellent breakfast, a good set off for our 11 miles march into the Zulu valley which we reached about 5 p.m. finding our tents pitched and Tea prepared. Our guard built us up a glorious fire on the road and when it got dark we sat alongside it on the bank and Lel got out his book on the stars and we did our best to identify them, while a pretty picture was made a little way off by our Sepoys and Nagas round another glorious fire, and the river made its pretty, soothing music just beyond. Sibboo and Assimoo are treasures of servants on the march, I must say, the food arrangements excellent in the former's hands, and the latter so handy and ready, lending a hand to everything, so quiet, and withal always so clean and smart. Our old friend, Ino Ram, who was Orderly to us on our Henema tour, is with us again, such an excellent fellow, big, fat and good-natured, and very handy, knowing all our ways. E 2,800ft.

10th Cheswajuma. Started a little before 10 a.m. taking the same route for about 5 miles as we did in our Xmas tour, then at the top of the hill turned to the left (N. by E) instead of to the right and made our way by a good bridle path down 900ft to the Siju, crossed by a very nice iron bridge, 200ft lower than the Zulu valley where we camped last night. Just the other side, in a shady spot, we found breakfast laid out and ready for us, the usual delicious camp stew! and etceteras. Since then our way has been steady up hill for 7 miles, endless zig-zags carrying us up the steep hillside, very pretty in parts, and the view over this wonderful land of hills growing finer and finer as we mounted. We got in about 4.30 to find a very tidy little two roomed bungalow, with a neat little flower garden outside, and a number of Ghenna stones picturesquely scattered round about. After tea we climbed up to the village and up onto one of those rough wooden platforms which the Nagas like so much, where they sit together, admire the view, talk and drink their zu. The view must be simply glorious from there but we were a little late.

Ms Ingram and CMS in village

Now we are enjoying the comfort of a huge wood fire and our attentive Naga Chaukidar in his pretty Angami dress, has brought us a monumental supply of timber to keep it up, it fills a fair portion of our little mud floored quarters!

11th Satajuma. E 5,900. Got off about 10 a.m. a glorious morning with a fresh "nip" in the air which was accounted for by the thick hoar frost which we found on the sheltered side of the hill. Our way lay fairly level and high up, passing through Chajubama village, empty apparently but for old crones and children, the men all out as we found later fetching in their loads of raw cotton, and so on till we arrived at Yarabama about 1 p.m. where we found breakfast laid out in the village and which we discussed before an admiring and wondering crowd. From there our line was mostly uphill till we reached this about 3 p.m., a little one roomed bungalow of the simplest build, planted on the top of a bare, windswept ridge, and windy it is, and cold! 48 degrees in the verandha when we arrived. We have a fire place, with a tin pipe chimney run out of the back of it, which by no means carries off the smoke from the piles of wood which are kept burning, so we sit close to the fire, with the door wide open, and keep up an accompaniment to our conversation in blowing one's nose and mopping our eyes. Sibboo, good man, has surpassed himself with an excellent batch of bread made yesterday under all the difficulties of the march – such a weight off my mind when the bread turns out well! to say nothing of our <u>chests</u>!

12th Killonassa, E. 6,100. A sixteen mile march through most beautiful and grand forest, magnificent trees, many must have been fully 120ft high; beautiful tree ferns too, and a very handsome sort of cane different to what we have seen before. A short distance out of Satujuma we passed over the site of Terocheswemi an old deserted Angami village situated on the crown of a hill 6,300ft, deserted some 7 years ago on account of some epidemic. Half way here we halted at Zulhama for breakfast which we found ready for us in the verandah of the little travellers' bungalow. At Satajuma we entered into the non-revenue paying country, country only under Political Control, and at Zulhama we said goodbye to the Angamis, and have now entered the Sema country. They are not nearly so smart and clean looking a people as the Angamis, in fact appearances seem altogether neglected. One peculiarity about them is the curious wads of cotton wool which they stick in their ears and then spread out into a wide fan shape of several inches depth each side of the face, and which has a very weird effect. The people about these hills have a curious legend that far away towards Burma there is a village of <u>women</u> only, a terrible and awful place! History (?) tells of some rashly enterprising travelling "bagmen" of this country having at rare intervals tempted fate by going there, but they never got back again! Also there is a legend of the existence of a man-eating tribe somewhere out in the "faraway" from here. Lel shot a very fine pine martin on the way, a lovely black coat and bushy tail, with cream coloured chest. We saw some Toucans also, but got no shot at them. From here you get a fine view of Wokka peak which, with its slanting lines of strata looking rather like a path, the natives call "the pathway of the Dead", their belief being, among the Aohs and Lotas, that all their dead must pass up and over this peak; in the same way that the Tonkals have a similar belief about their mountain Servi, they believe all their dead must go up that. At the top stands the Guardian of their heaven, who demurs about the entrance of the stranger. But the friends of the departed, in the funeral ceremonies, are enumerating his virtues and pronouncing him worthy, and sacrificing a buffalo for his advantage, so the Guardian listens, and the buffalo pushing the door open with his horns, the stranger gets into his heaven at last alright.

13th Sataka. E. 5,250. A 13 mile march brought us here about 4.30, the first part through forest like yesterday's march, but the last 5 miles on open hillside. About a mile out a deputation from this village, and its neighbor, Kukiye, met us, such a weird collection; white haired old Sataka in his red cloth, and other headmen of both villages and a crowd besides, all eager to see us, and to get us to visit their respective villages and with screeching fowls tucked under their arms as offerings and all talking and jabbering one against the other. After drinking some of the inevitable zu we got off again, one of the newcomers whose rollicking, rolling gait, and breezy manner suggested his having had quite enough of that exhilarating drink as was good for him picked me up in my basket chair and ran off with me down the rest of the hill, the tribe following, and deposited me at the bungalow with a flourish. We were soon settled down, made an excellent tea, and were cosing comfortably over the fire, Lel smoking and I lying down reading, when in looked Hooli and said "There is a fire, Sahib" in ordinary quiet tones. "Where's the fire?" says Lel. "In the bungalow" was the reply. "By Jove, yes" says Lel, as we looked up there were the flames showing through the roof just over the fire place.

'Sataka bungalow after the fire' 13 January 1901

Then what a scrimmage ensued! Each seized their bedding and flung it outside, the alarm spread and up came "the army" (our six dear little sepoys) and the work of clearing everything out was soon done, and the tent also in which the Budlet was located dropped down on her, and but for Leslie's rushing in, on the lamp and the candle inside it too, when there would have been another conflagration! and in less than 20 minutes there we were roofless on the hillside, with all our possessions strewn in chaotic confusion around us. Such a weird scene it was, the splendid blaze of the woodwork and thatch, with the wild hordes of savages who immediately swarmed down from the village, rushing and dancing about in the fire light, scattering water and shouting at the tops of their voices. Bubby and Khalu took it all with beautiful calmness. They curled themselves up on the first blanket and slept through the whole business. As may be supposed it took a long time to find all our possessions again, but we did at last, our food, among other things being found in the oddest places. The devoted Hooli was seen prosecuting an endless search up and down the hillside with a whisp of lighted grass to help him, always searching, but never finding apparently, and when asked what he was looking for it came out that this was one <u>salt spoon</u>! which was missing and it is the only thing, together with its salt cellar which has been lost. Our chef, Sibboo, showed himself the true artist in his line! Nothing disturbed him from the <u>cooking of his dinner</u>! An occasional glance outside was enough, and then he was back again with his pots. When all was over, and a new bit of ground levelled, the tent was put up again, B.'s and my bed put in it, and a tiny table in the middle, and we all sat down to dinner about 9.30, a bit tired, and very glad soon after, to get to bed, Lel doubling up with "the Army". It was a little pathetic to see, the last thing before we turned in, amid the blackened posts of

'Headman at Jekia's village – Sema Nagas'

the poor little ruin, the fire still burning merrily in the fire place, the only thing left, round which we had been sitting so cosily only 3 hours before!

14th We halted today at Sataka and started off this morning about 10, to go to Jekia's village about 4 miles off over the hills on the opposite side of the valley in the Independent country. And <u>what</u> miles those were 4 were! I could not walk, not being very fit, so had 3 mighty men from the village told off bearing me in my basket, and what breakneck places they carried me over – along bridges made of fallen trees, slippery with weeds and wet, over great trunks

'Sema Nagas at Jekia's village'

of trees blocking the way, and up steep places which required some climbing to get over unburdened, but which they took me over with next to no trouble at all. Six Semas went on in front and cleared the jungle, cutting notches for footing with their daos, and so improved the path for us a little. At last we got to Jekia's, over the crest of the hill, and then what a grand view we had, as we sat down over our breakfast in front of the Goanbura's house. Down below us was the valley of the Tizu, with Kiaku's village this side of it and to our left, which Lel and Capt. Cole burned[1] in '98 for refractory conduct. On the other side of the Tizu rose another big range, with Loshianpu's and Vikia's villages on its crest, also visited by Lel then, with Gobische's village just the other side where also is the valley of the Zita, while in the far distance, beyond a further range we caught sight of Lel's "Mecca", Sarametti, its features quite plainly visible through the field glasses, as yet unvisited by any European, but the aim and desire of all Lel's longings! A great number of other villages were to be seen from there and among them Inatu, renowned and feared on account of the belief the natives have that its headman and his wife have the power of turning themselves at will into <u>Tigers</u>! Breakfast over and having taken in as much of this view into this wild and independent country as was possible, we started homewards again with our picturesque following of Savages, in coloured clothes (those who <u>had</u> clothes!) with spears and daos, greatly increased their and my carriers' spirits rising as we neared home and finding vent in wild war whoops and got in again by about 5, having had a delightful and most interesting outing. Tonight is quiet and peaceful, no fire alarms! and no barking deer or Sambur even, calling as yesterday.

15th Gukia's. E 4,300. 3½ miles. The coolies that came to take our loads this morning were I think the very <u>dirtiest</u> crew I've ever seen. One rather exceeded all the others, so Ino Ram caught him by his hair and dragging him up to a bucket of water standing by, forced his head down into it, obliging him thus to wash his face. Seeing he didn't resent it I ordered the 3 men told off bearing me to do the same, and they set to work at it quite cheerfully, scraping each others faces also with bits of cane to assist in getting off some of the crust, but even these measures did not succeed in making them <u>clean</u>, only a little less thickly black than before. We started by going up into Sataka's village above our camp, a poor little village but having the most curious ornamentations in

---

1. 'In November (1897) we had a small punitive tour against Kiaku, a Sema village in the Upper Tizu valley whose men had raided across and taken heads from our side of the border, which then ran practically along the line of the old Sema political control road through Cheswjunu – Sataka – Eniloni – to Mokokchung. Cole, self, and a sporting planter friend Wright from Moriani and 50 rifles formed our party. I marched straight across country from Kohima via Wokani and Nuonomi, met Cole and Wright at Ghuckia's village, then we crossed the high eastern range at Zinittum's, and descended early one bitter cold morning on Kiaku which with glasses we saw was full of armed Semas. A thick mist however blew up the valley under cover of which they thought better than to oppose us, and vanished. The village was empty when we reached it and three days were spent in searching the neighbourhood, confiscating cattle, grain etc. before burning the place, and we then crossed the valley visiting Lhoshimpu and Sakai, returning to Kohima in mid-December'. (LWS, *Memoir*. 1926).

it, enormously high bamboo rods covered over with leaves tied round them, and standing in rows like gigantic fishing rods, with dangling ornaments at their ends. These are set up to commemorate feasts in connection with the getting in of the harvest. The people are a miserable, low, dirty looking lot, but are surpassed by those of Momi, another little village we passed through about ½ mile beyond Sataka's – who are dirty beyond words in their habitations, surroundings, persons, and such rags of clothing as some of them aspired to wearing.

'Chief's House Ghukia's Village N Sema Nagas'

From here our road went continually downhill to the valley of the Lunka, the foliage growing lovely as we approached the river bed. The "Sago" palms about here are <u>most</u> beautiful; some that we saw yesterday had leaves which could not have been less than from 25 to 30ft long by 15ft wide. We had our breakfast by the roadside just the other side of the pretty little bridge and then started on the somewhat hot and tedious climb up here. As we approached this a following of men and little urchins all armed with spears gathered behind us, headed by Gukia himself and his little boy, who ushered us into the village, all the rest of the inmates (a very dirty lot too!) swarming out to see us pass. And first of all we had to go to Gukia's house where he made us sit down while his chief wife (he had 3 we found, and 14 children!) waited on us and gave us Zu, a lady of colossal proportions dressed in a short cloth round her waist, and a huge and handsome necklace of agates, cornelians and shells etc.

'Ghuckia's village'

It was a very picturesque interior, the darkness usual to all these houses lit up by a large fire on the ground in the centre of the back compartment, pots cooking on it, and surmounted by a platform raised on 4 tall thick posts, Gukia seated in the pride of master of the house, with his son beside him; Mrs G., No. 1, passing to and fro, busy waiting on us or hovering about to look at our clothes etc., my gloves and my watch being special marvels, while the background was a shadowy mass of tightly packed humanity gazing their fill at us from a respectful distance. Then to the little bungalow and Tea, after which we took a stroll round the village to pick out places for photos to be taken in the morning.

16th Emilomi. E. 4,700. 8 ½ miles. Began our day by taking photos, a doubtful, cloudy day, so we have some fears for their success; then off on our way about 10.30, our road taking us first about 2,000ft down to the Gileki where beside the bridge we found our breakfast and then up 3,000ft to this another Sema village, but the people not quite so fearfully dirty looking as the last.

Deputations as usual came out from Sakomi which we passed on the way, from Limitsasni close by here, and from this, headmen in red cloths and others carrying spears, all of whom, after the presentation of Zu and fowls, tailed in behind us making quite a formidable procession.

'Emilomi'

This is a little one-roomed bungalow, mud floor, mud walls, and a highly ventilated roof, but it is something to have a roof at all! and we are <u>very</u> cautious with the fire! It is a grand position, and the view should be glorious, only today it is cloudy and the air is full of smoke now from the jhooming which is going on. We took a walk up the village which is very picturesque built on a hill, with bamboos clustering about it, drank Zu in the Goanbura's house, took photos and sketched, and then came back to Tea and rest.

17th <u>Auchakilimi</u>. E. 5,500ft. 10½ miles. Our road today took us up over a shoulder of Pipliakami, 6,100ft high, the watershed between the basins of the Doyang and the Dikku, and from there gradually downhill to this, a rather uninteresting road, the hillsides being all bare, ready for the "Job's Tear" (Kunkri dhan) crop. We passed by Segomi and Serami rather notable villages on the

'Emilomi village El. 6000'

'Lhoshiapu - Sema chief'

other side of the valley. At the former two unfortunate traders from near Wokka who visited it a little while ago, were taken prisoners, both were tortured and one eventually had his head cut off, while the other was kept tied up on a machan from beneath which they smoked him with burning chillis. Fortunately however while they were feasting and drinking over the taking of the head of the other poor wretch, this one escaped, brought in information, and in due time punishment was meted out in the burning of their village. Just beyond Segomi are the 4 big villages of Satami which have never yet been visited, a somewhat turbulent lot, who frequently send in cheeky messages of defiance to the Powers in Kohima. Serami is a huge village, spreading in several detached portions over the ridge on which it is located, and is the old parent village of this and other neighbouring villages. This border land from all accounts appears a ticklish neighbourhood; there is no knowing when one or other of the turbulent villages across the border and beyond our control may not break out and go raiding and head hunting, and then if damage is done among those within our Control, punishment <u>has</u> to be meted out to them, and this not infrequently is found advisable also when the damage is confined to the other side of the border, for unpunished crime so near at hand has a bad effect and tends to lawlessness among the neighbouring villages within our Control, necessitating more punitive expeditions. One notices how all through this border country all the people on the roads carry spears, and generally daos also, the former always beautifully bright and sharp bladed, in great contrast to those of the Angamis and other people under our direct rule, where all is assured peace, and whose spears being now only ornaments are invariably dull, rusty and blunt. It has been a dull day and by the time we got here, 3 p.m., had turned quite cold. We took a turn through the village, but saw nothing very interesting or remarkable, though it is a prettily situated village on three knolls with Bamboos scattered through it. The cold drove us home and we are glad to sit over the fire. There was a funny little incident before our start this morning which made us all laugh. Our Coolies appeared more filthy than words can say, so our stalwart orderly Ino Ram, grinning broadly, laid forcible hands on the worst, caught them by their hair and dragged them up to a bucket of water and made them wash before they took up their loads; they struggled and resisted, but it was no good, Ino held them fast, and amid the laughter and jeers of everyone all round, including their own comrades, they were not allowed to go till severe scrubbing had made them comparatively clean! <u>Never</u> have I seen anything to equal their dirt! but they are sturdy and strong though of no great stature.

Untitled

18th Lemoni. E. 4,050 A grey and cold morning, and we had not gone far on our way before down came the rain in drenching floods, which soon got through our clothes to a certain extent and made the road which is very clayey extremely slippery, while the wind was bitter. Luckily it passed off soon, and the sun came out again to cheer and dry us. We passed by the village and deserted bungalow of Chichemi, the scene of one of Leslie's early experiences when he first came to Kohima and which he described to us on the spot. – On his arrival there he found the ground round the bungalow occupied by a crowd of men armed with their tall shields and daos, somewhat excited and looking as though got up for some "tamasha". From the Bungalow the ground descended to a little saddle and on a corresponding knoll beyond it was a corresponding body of men from the next village. From the man in charge who spoke Hindustani only very haltingly, Lel gathered that these two villages were going to celebrate a yearly sort of contest for some bit of ground, an amicable sort of tamasha, and being asked if he wished to stop it said, "Oh no! let them go on, I should like to see it"! So both sides began a most picturesque war dance, then with a sudden rush down hill approached each other on the saddle below. Here they again resumed their dance, gradually drawing nearer and nearer to each other and getting more and more excited and finally coming into collision. Then as Lel sat up on the bank he saw that something more than <u>fun</u> was going on; a man ran back by him with his eye cut, and a woman with her breast open, while troops of women on both sides rushed down with their clothes full of stones which they lobbed up into the air over the shields and onto the heads of the opposing parties, and Lel realized that it was a bona fide <u>fight</u> that was in progress; and that should one side prevail with any decided success it was more than probable that in the heat of having tasted blood they would turn upon him and his little escort, so taking the Chowkidar and another man he rushed down between them, laying about with his stick and so drove

'Lota warrior charging'

them apart, while the rest of his guard who had been at their food, having got the alarm, came down and joined him, and so at last they got them to separate, after which he called the leaders out and discussed the cause of quarrel with them and so brought matters to a conclusion. But it was very nearly being a bad business and stones were flying heavily in all directions when he went into the fray, and daos were out too. – From there we came on to Alopvomi, where we found the faithful Assimoo and Hooli had got our breakfast ready for us in front of a village house, with comfortable seats on thick bundles of thatching grass ranged up for us. A picturesque village but the usual <u>awfully</u> dirty people, all except one baby which I spotted, a jolly, friendly little mite, quite willing to come to me and be nursed, though I think his mother, a young girl, was happier when she got him back again! Our 10 mile march seemed wonderfully short today, and we got in quite early, before 3 p.m., but then it was nearly all downhill, which makes a difference. Yesterday and today we are enjoying the luxury of a two-roomed bungalow, with the tent for dining in, so we spread ourselves out!

'Lemomi Rest house'

True, the floors are only mud, and not too dry either, and the doors and windows are not noted for their capacity for shutting, or the roof for its power of keeping out the light and the wind! but we still <u>have</u> a roof, and <u>walls</u>, and a fire place, and space and on the whole make ourselves very comfortable. We took a walk in the village, but it is uninteresting and the people more and <u>more dirty</u> beyond description! An industry of this part is the making of clay ghurrahs, which the people make and mould most cleverly entirely with the hand. They use them in place of the wooden and bamboo vessels which are what the Angamis and others make for themselves.

20th Mokokchung. We got in here yesterday afternoon about 4, having started about 11 a.m. in pouring wet and under a sky that looked absolutely hopeless. At first we thought of halting for the day at Lemoni and waiting for better weather, but food supplies were low, no bread left, and we were anxious to get our letters after being without them so long, so finally we decided to face the weather whatever it might be and started, and happily after about 2 hours marching we gradually got out of it and for the rest of the way had it fine, but so bitterly cold! especially where we got onto the saddle of the hill where the wind was very high. Walking too was a considerable effort, the soil being stiff clay which caked heavily on one's boots, but was necessary to keep at all warm. Breakfast on the way was of course impossible, but the Goorkha Officer here, fat old Subedar Sunjai, sent a man out with milk to meet us, and with that and a slice of bread and butter fished out of the jhapa the cravings of hunger were kept off till we got in. About 3 miles out we turned off to go through Uhngma village, a very big one which had been 2 thirds burnt down the night before. What was left of it was <u>most</u> picturesque, but the desolation of the other part was pitiable to behold. Built on a rocky ridge there was nothing but the bare rock left heaped up with ashes and a few charred remains of their household implements the solidity of which, cut out of single huge blocks of timber, had checked their total destruction before the rain came down and prevented the fire from spreading further.

'Mokok'

Already some of the poor sufferers had got up new thatched shelters, and the people from this village and others near will help them with timber, thatching grass and labour to get straight again for these people are very good to one another in trouble. Jolly glad we were to get in at last, I must say! and to get a meal and we had looked forward keenly to the comforts of a <u>fire</u> and we piled on the logs in both rooms and when the smoke came up we said cheerfully "Oh it's only at first, the chimney will get warm soon and then it will be <u>all</u> right!" but was it? The door was set open, and then a window, then another window, and then an opposite door and still we coughed and choked, and blew our noses and mopped our eyes, and were driven forth shivering in our great coats into the windy verandha to get a little respite for our eyes and lungs; and yet we could not let the fires out for there were clothes and things to be dried after the wet march and so with groans we had to face the smoke and get on as well as we could through dinner and the interval before bed time, which was all much too painful to allow of any thought of writing diaries up to date. Today wind and sun happily make us independent of fires and our surroundings have that usual curious aspect when circumstances make it desirable that everything should have an "airing"! <u>All</u> the contents of bed valises and Gladstones are festooned around on all available palings and bushes, to say nothing of the results of sundry amateur "washes", a truly curious effect! We took a walk around the "Lady's Mile" in the evening – such a glorious sunset and so wonderfully clear after the rain.

21st Mokokchung. Mr. Williamson turned up to breakfast and all the rest of the morning we were busy at work over letters, a big dak having come in last evening, the accumulations of ten days. Have settled my passage in "Imperatrix" Austrian Lloyd for March 1st which seems dreadfully near now – it will be horrid leaving dear old Lel behind, and the little home at Kohima. It has been so windy and cold today we hunted out a sheltered and sunny nook to sit in down near the road, taking books and work after breakfast, but Lel proved independent of either taking out his leisure in a peaceful snooze. Then up to a most excellent Tea with Mr. Williamson, and a tour of inspection of the site of his new house on the very top of the hill, a beautiful but most windy position, a chat over his fire with cheering "varieties" and back home to dinner at which he joined us, a weeping party again reduced to tears and sniffs by the clouds of smoke which make our evenings here so comfortless.

22nd Another English mail in today with news of Wyn and the Xmas doings at Lil's – jolly times for the children. Lel and Mr. W. gone off to Mongsemdi where L. has to inspect his guard, and now in the p.m. B. and I are making cakes, and supplies of butter for the rest of our tour. Butter abounds here! and it's a great treat to get it so good. We make it in our toilet basins, wash and salt it well and put it down in Bamboo Chungas where it will keep for weeks.

'Mokok'

We've got a little "Mirrie" dog brought in to take to Mr. Ward (44th) and have just given him a bath, through which he yelled lustily, and now fastened to my bed near the fire he is continuing the same sort of song, distracting and deafening, only stopping when he is nursed. Later went to call on the wife of the worthy road Babu here, Prolade, a funny experience rather; were ushered in by Prolade to an enclosure with high fencing all round, the lady being "Purdah Nashin" and found her there with her friend the Dr. Babu's wife, a nice intelligent woman busy with the sort of little farmyard they'd got there. Mrs. P. a very nice looking but desperately shy woman took us inside and gave us seats and then we had to talk! a very difficult business not being very "glib" in the language, having no common subjects to talk about, and our hostess being much too shy to speak a word! However the children and the other lady, less shy, provided some means for getting along somehow and our hostess presented us with Cigarettes the smoking of which filled up the one or two dead pauses which the situation unavoidably involved! Still I think our visit gave them great pleasure, at least they said so, and looked it when we were leaving, and no doubt they will talk of it for weeks to come. Prolade met us outside with a funny little speech of apology, hoping we would excuse it if they had made any mistakes in deportment, for they were not used to visitors but I think he too was proud of his wife having had visitors, a thing, I fancy, which had never happened before.

23rd Nunkum. B. and I started about 11 and had a very pleasant cool march, breakfast half-way and got in about 4 p.m. Lel coming in later having done the whole distance from Mongsemdi, 26 miles, straight off. A most wonderful and glorious sunset, this sea of hills first golden, then crimson as if on fire. Tumsi turned up and his brother, and we were pestered all the evening by houris coming in to sell things. Bought some of their wonderful earrings.

'Nankum'

24th Halted. Went out in the morning and took two sketches, Lel and B also taking photos of the big moranghurs at the end of the village and other street views. It is bitterly cold, very grey and has looked like rain all day. B. and Lel went for a walk in the p.m. to get warm while I attempted a somewhat ambitious sketch of the lower end of the village, rather beyond my powers I'm afraid. Tumsi and his two boys came up in the evening and made a pretty group sitting over our fire while the little kids discussed the sweets we gave them. More bevies of houris, little full grown women not up to my shoulder sometimes, filling our room and trying to get enormous prices for sundry small wares.

'War Drum,[2] Nunkum'

25th Lungtyan. Eleven miles all down hill, the first part very steep indeed, about 800 ft. in less than ¼ mile. Lel took a photo of the graves as we passed. On our way we had to pass a big jhoom fire raging and roaring, its flames and clouds of smoke coming right up to the road. Looking through the stems of trees and grass down into the glare of fire below was like a glimpse in the Inferno. Got in early and went up into the village, a poor little place and dirty looking like all Sema villages. Don't know what Sibboo is about with the bread – he is presenting us nowadays with petrifications which almost require an axe to cut them, and when cut they disclose nothing but a large hole inside, not exactly satisfying to hunger!

2.	This drum is of the same style and model, if not the same drum, as that sketched by Woodthorpe in the 1875.(Woodthorpe, *Notes*. 1882).

'Namkum Moranghurs, or Club houses, for the young men'

'Corner in Lungtiang Village (Sema)'

Tour to Mokokchung via Ghukia's Village – *January 1901* | **141**

'Lungtyan Sema'

'Doyang bridge'

26th Koyo. Three miles more down hill, down to the Doyang[3] bridge where Lel took a photo and then 7 miles up to this, a rather uninteresting marching, and rather monotonous with its many zig-zags. Got in by soon after 2 p.m. and after settling in went up through the village and took some photos; it is picturesque and the only Lota village we pass through. It is wonderfully clean but the houses are extremely small and cramped looking. Our Tea has brought to light more petrifications, but the cakes made at Mokok are good, and His Excellency is pleased to approve! The little Mirrie dog we are taking in to George Ward has turned out a little dear – a most sweet and taking nature, and full of fun and has quite attached himself to us. I should like to keep him now!

'Wokha fort'

27th Wokka. An 8 mile march which brought us in about 12.30. Before starting the dak came in, bringing the terrible news[4] of the Queen's death, a great shock to us, as we had heard nothing of any illness or anxiety about her. It was odd that as we watched the man coming up with the dak, a sight we generally welcome with pleasure, it flashed across me "I wonder what bad news he is bringing, I wish he weren't coming". Coming over the ridge we were met by the American missionary Babu who seems to have an easy time, with 9 con-

---

3. The suspension bridge was first erected in 1899. (Archer, *Journey.* 1947).

verts,[5] and 3 assistants to help him teach them. Our breakfast was a bit calamitous today. We came in very wholesomely hungry and sat down keenly to our camp stew, but the first mouthful showed its reigning flavour to be kerosene, and His Excellency starting up in horror, and appealing loudly to Sibboo, the Chef and purveyor of the feast, on the latter's appearance plate, implements and contents were hurled at that erring individual. It turned out that the lamps and kerosene supply had been packed <u>on the top</u> of the potatoes which had got duly anointed during the shaking of the march! There was a noble row all round of course and then we settled down to tinned fare of which we keep a supply in case of accidents. Our "pink-mouthed hooligan", the last addition to our menagerie, is a great and most favoured pet, allowed to sleep on beds and to do all sorts of things never allowed before, and is generally spoiled all round. But one can't help it – he is such a fascinating little thing.

'Temakodima' bungalow

---

4.   Queen Victoria had died five days earlier, on 22nd January 1901.

5.   Despite the sound relationship and cooperation between British officials and the missionaries Connie's attitude toward the latter does not appear to be that positive. She mentions them twice and makes no comment on the Rivenbergs in Kohima whom she knew. It is probable she was unaware of Butler's earlier rhetorical question 'Who shall say that the Bible will not be the means of changing the habits and ideas of these wild savages?' (Butler. *Travels and Adventures.* 1855: Sema, *British Policy*, 1991).

'Temakodima' village

28th Temakodina. (Rengmas) An 18 mile march with breakfast half way at Kotsama, and got in here soon after 5 p.m. But our day began with a most exciting incident. We seem to have a fatality in being concerned with <u>fires</u>, and this morning we assisted at a most noble one, the burning down of the Wokka Post and General Civil Office. We were just going to sit down to our early breakfast before starting, having got up extra early in view of the long march we had before us, when we saw smoke coming out of this house about 500 yds off, and then all the community of the little place with Lel leading hurried down to the scene, B. and I taking our Cameras to take "shots" of the various effects we might see! It was a wonderful sight, the fire having started in the verandah where all the papers, Govt. records etc. were kept; the smoke was awful, making it almost impossible to approach the house to save things. By degrees a heterogeneous collection of extraordinary goods of sorts, the possessions of the Babu, Jadob Bindha, were dragged out and scattered abroad and some chests of papers etc. The flames were <u>grand</u>, as all the woodwork in these houses is saturated with kerosene oil to preserve it from damp and insects. The poor Babu in charge (his "Bos" the above Babu being away) was a pitiable object of despair and distraction, appealing to Lel to bear witness that it was not his fault, his English becoming more and more hopelessly unintelligible as he feelings grew more and more overwrought.

'Mithun and group in Themakodima village (Rengma)'

'Mithun speared for a feast'

'Wokha Post Office' January 1901

Tour to Mokokchung via Ghukia's Village – January 1901 | **147**

'Wokha Post Office burnt down' January 1901

"Sir, what I possibly doing can? Records, Govt. papers, house burning, and I occupied, busy there. Great punishment waiting for me, all saying Babu's fault, but how Babu's fault when I, Babu, not there". And then falling at Lel's feet (when the latter was helping him to write some report of it) and clasping him round the knees, with plenteous sobs, "You are not D.C. but you commanding, you King, not King, but almost God!, you good words saying, pleasant words – how I saving anything possible, when I away over there" etc. etc! Lel of course reassured him and will do his best for him. We waited on, taking very "snapshots" till the roof fell in, and then went back to breakfast, and started, B. and I, leaving Lel to help the poor Babu out with his report and follow us.

29th Nerahma. A 17 mile march, started about 10, had lunch half way, and got in about 4 p.m. Before starting went up into the village where Lel took photos of mitton and of Guason and little Johnnie who is looking much heartier than when we saw him last, while I did a sketch of the Moranghur. The day began very hot, but it is cold enough here and we are glad of our fires.

30th Tessima. Only 4½ miles today but of these 2½ were as nearly perpendicular as could be. For ¾ of an hour we dropped down hill, obliged to keep our eyes fixed on the ground to pick every step, our hobnailed shoes finding little hold on the tumbled mass of rocks and stones which chiefly formed the track, and then from the river bed at the bottom proceedings were reversed. Lel and I stayed on here for the night, B. going on after breakfast into Kohima. Went on with my sketches, and looked over the gardens etc. with Lel. It is a dear little place and I am glad they have not yet begun to pull the little house down for repairs, so that we can have one day more here before I go. Not far off, and about 9 miles from Kohima on the Wokka road, is one of the few remains supposed to have been left by the Burmese as a memorial of their invasion when they swept through these hills in 1823. A large stone with a Peacock cut on it and standing on one of the hills is said to mark the halting place of some great Burmese general and his army.

'Temakodima Guason'

31st Kohima. A glorious morning, we got in here by about 1 p.m. coming the short way by the Naga path and taking a couple of photos of the pretty little Naga house on the way. About ½ way we met the little "pink-mouthed Hooligan" stumping his way back to Tessima! having broken loose from Eno Ram! so we tied him up with the halter till we met Eno again, searching for him! and who took him once more in charge. Such a greeting from our little "Mirri" who has grown a lot and is looking lovely and from our own dear little "Bunder-long". He and the Mirrie have made great friends, and it is the sweetest thing to see them playing together. – Tennis and Tea at the Club and billiards afterwards.

Tour to Mokokchung via Ghukia's Village – *January 1901* | **149**

'Tesima bungalow'

'Our house Kohima'

Chapter 7

Kohima and Dimapur
February 1901

Feb. 1st Met Lel down in the Lines in the p.m. to go round the Lines with him for the adjudging of his prize for the tidiest Barrack and best garden. None of the 44th could come to assist on the Committee as they'd had a long field day, so Sergeant Dorward and Mrs. Tolley made up the party.

'Kohima from the gate'

'Kohima warrior in festal dress. Each feather represents a Head which has been cut off by the wearer. Feathers of the tail of the Toucan'.

The Lines, and Married Lines, were quite a show, a credit to the battalion, but we were all pleased at dear old Arjun's company coming in a long way first, but eventually tying with Jamalluddin, so they both got a "1st Prize". It was nice to hear from Tolley also what high commendation the P.M.O. had expressed on the Lines and their conditions when he had inspected them a few days ago. Lel takes an immensity of trouble over them and one likes to know it is appreciated.

2nd Viletia came to ask for a tiger skin to take away to make up into a shield, which he would use for one day, he said, for his Ghenna festival and then give back to Lel. He is a splendid man so I took his photo. In the p.m. took Tea out about 2½ miles on the Khonoma road to meet Lel on his way back. Some Nagas passed us carrying Toucans and Hooluks which they had killed.

3rd Sunday. Took Tea out about 3 miles up the Manipur road to meet Lel coming from Kuzama. A cold and windy day, but found a sheltered little hole below the road. Just as Lel arrived, for some unknown reason "Bubby" wantonly dug his teeth into the leg of an unfortunate Naga passing, just cutting a vein, and the bleeding was terrible. We bound it up with strips of duster and eventually with the Drahby's help he joined some comrades who took him off to his home at Phesima. They are to send in for remedies tomorrow from the hospital – with those and Lel's 2 or 3 rupees the man won't mind much.

'Sibboo our cook and Japoli in their war paint. (Samaguting village)'. Kohima

4th Mr. Kennedy is very seedy – has been bad with bronchitis, all the fault of that owl of a Doctor, Dr. Weinman, who let him get up and go about when he had got fever on him and was actually spitting blood. To the tender mercies of such idiots are we committed here! I've been doctoring him a bit and having turned the corner I hope he'll get on now.

6th Wednesday. B. and I went and called on the Rivenbergs, and then on Miss Kerr, with whom I left B. to have Tea. Came home to tea with Lel and then went for a walk round the Lady's Mile.

'Entrance to our house, Manipur cart road to right'

7th Thursday. Sent up tea to the club and had some Tennis, and billiards after.

8th Friday. Had a bit of a walk with Lel. Mr. Ward and Mr. Grant dined.

9th Saturday. The Kerrs gave Tea at the Tennis.

10th Sunday. Lel and I strolled round Capt. Wood's garden and the Club and took photos and another from the Fort Hill. Took a turn in the p.m. and came in early to develop photos.

12th Tuesday. A dull, cold day. Had a nice breezy walk with Lel up Kohima hill, then down onto the road below.

13th Wednesday. The weather has changed to wet with high winds which get up at all hours of the day and night, setting doors and windows banging in a most disturbing way. We have got to dine at Mess, as Regimental Guests, and it is pouring wet and so cold. Would much rather sit round our cosy fire here than go out a mile down a muddy road for our dinner, and back again <u>uphill</u> which is perhaps the worst part of it!

'In front of our house. Sibboo, wife, wife's friend, his boy. Our servants' houses'

14th Thursday. Our dinner last night was <u>most</u> festive and we enjoyed it immensely. We luckily got down dry without rain and found that all the station, including the Rivenbergs, were invited. The table had been laid in the ante-room to allow of its extension, and it was looking prettier than I had ever seen it before with all their plate out, and so nicely lighted. I had Col. Molesworth one side and Mr. Kennedy the other and was well off.

'Kohima village'

'Dhan (rice) pounding festival Kohima' 1901

After dinner Mr. Ward did some "willing" with B. and then we returned to the large dining room where they said they'd show us the game of "Hicockolorum" and they did! I never saw a more animated game! And there were not a few bruises as its results! Paid our P.P.Cs this afternoon, Lel joining us, and dine tonight at Mr. Kennedy's.

15th Friday. Had a very pleasant evening yesterday; the Kerrs, Mr. Ward and Col. Molesworth. The latter is quite a new man since he has heard he will get his 2 years extension of command and is excellent company and dear little Mr. Kennedy is a most perfect host. Champagne flowed and B.s and my health and "bon voyage" were drunk. This p.m. we had a jolly walk, Lel taking us up the Kuki picket hill from the Lady's Mile and then down and home by the Cart road. A most lovely day, so clear after the rain, the views perfect and the sunset beautiful. Went out to say goodbye to Mrs. Tolley first and joined Lel at office, then home to tea and walk after it. Got all our carts off this morning with all our luggage and dine tonight with Mr. K. again, so that servants and kit can go on.

Kohima and Dimapur – *February 1901* | 157

'Angami Nagas pounding rice in full war paint at the Dhan pounding festival' Kohima

'Dhan (rice) pounding festival Kohima' 1901

16th A very cheery evening yesterday, Col. M. and Mr. Ward making up the party. This morning Col. M. Mr. Grant and Mr. Pritchard came up to see us start. It was horrid having to leave and feeling one was going away to leave Lel behind for so long, but one had to make the best of it and get through as cheerfully as one could. "Viletia" brought the tiger skin shield to show us, beautifully done up and we photo'd him, then started off, our friends coming ½ a mile or so down the road with us. Mr. K. came all the way to Zubza where he gave us an excellent breakfast about 1 p.m. then on we started again at 3 p.m. and here we are now at Piphima 20 miles on our way.

17th Sunday. 20 miles to <u>Nichu Guard</u> Here we arrived about 4.30. Started this morning from Piphima about 9 and walked about 2½ miles, but the sun was hot and the road terribly dusty so there was not much enjoyment to be got out of it and B. and I therefore got into the trap and drove the rest of the way to Ghaspani where the usual stewpot and appliances had been left by Sibboo who had started at dawn with the carts. It is a pretty and cosy little bungalow and the rest and shade were welcome. Leslie came up in about ½ an hour, walking, and we then had breakfast, took a photo of the place and started on about 1.30, walking another 2 miles. After that the road was awful even for driving and we didn't get out of the trap again except to get photos of the "Kukipani" bridge, a fine bridge opened since we came up 14 months ago.

Kohima and Dimapur – *February 1901* | **159**

'Angami interpreters' Nihu in centre

'Cart road near Piphima' 1901

'Ghaspani – Rest house' February 1901

The scenery after that was lovely, a deep winding gorge with the river running through it, increased by the Chate, which bringing all the water drainage from Paona, joins the Kuki a little lower down. It was nice to get in and get some Tea after all the dust we'd been swallowing. This is a miserable little bungalow of 2 rooms, but most charmingly situated close to a pretty bend of the river whose water flows by with a most pleasant and soothing ripple under a deep bank only a few yards from the verandah. Up to 1896 there had been for many years a Guard of 50 men and a Stockade here. After Tea Lel and I climbed up the hill and traced out the markings of the old buildings and earth works and hoped to get a view of the sunset from above, but the jungle was too thick to allow of views though it was a nice walk. Our little Mirrie has been sent on always with the carts with the idea that the latter would save his puppy legs a bit. But he has no idea of going anyway but on his own feet and shrieked and yelled so when put in the cart, almost throttling himself in his efforts to get away from his chain, so that he had to be put down and allowed to foot it through but the process is visibly reducing the rotundity of his sides, though he is as cheeky and full of fun as ever, and not a bit tired.

18th Monday. Drove into Dimapur – started walking a couple of miles, but the dust was awful and were glad to get into the trap and stop there, Lel cantering about on his pony. We got in about noon and found Dr. Calthrop (generally known as "Old Cough-drop") and Dr. Leventon (who had been at Kohima

'Kuki Pani bridge' February 1901

'Nichuguard – Rest House' February 1901

with the 43rd) who both welcomed us all to a very good breakfast at the Dak Bungalow. The latter very prettily situated on a bank which surrounds a fine large tank. After breakfast I went out to photo the ruins, disclosed when the jungle was cleared for laying the line.

'Dimapur Tank – and bungalow' February 1901

'Dunsiri river at Dimapur' February 1901

No record exists of who were the builders and carvers of these ruins. Nothing is known. They are remains of Phallic worship and may be anything up to 2000 years old. From there we went on to the station (?) and brought away poor Bubby and Mirrie who were very miserable there tied up in the sun and went back to Tea; after which in the cool of the morning Lel and I took a turn in the Forest, a narrow track cut through its marvelous denseness. Had a great alarm later on that the Mirrie was lost, and sent messengers everywhere offering rewards for him but the independent little creature had just started off to go back to his friends at the station and was found and duly brought back all safe to our great satisfaction. About 10 p.m. we started off once more and arrived at the "station", packed ourselves away in a 3rd class compartment where we passed the night trying to sleep and not to be cold, reaching <u>Lumding</u> about 6 a.m. on the..

'Ancient monoliths in the ruined fort at Dimapur in the Nambor. Their origin and meaning is absolutely unknown' February 1901

19th Tuesday. Here we changed trains, and got into a 1st class and here we had to part from dear old Lel[1] and very hard it seemed. He is off on a tour through

---

1. 'In late March 1901 your mother and the Budlet [Miss Ingram *Ed.*] went to England travelling on a ballast train from Dimapur to Lumding where I saw them off. The trio biz had not been a success in its entirety – very few are, and all were relieved when it ended though there was no break in friendship'. (LWS, *Memoir*. 1926).

Dimapur Cachari monolith 1901

new country up to Henema, and so back to Kohima, and I am glad he has this interest to occupy him for these first few days of his lonely life again. The old "Cough-drop" was very good in entertaining us for our between whiles and it was very fairly cool all the way, till we reached Gauhati, about 4.30 p.m. Here our luggage was all taken on by the train down to the steamer while we went off to the Dak Bungalow, an uncommonly good one, and had an excellent dinner, ordered beforehand by wire, and then drove down to the ghat, found our steamer and all our luggage duly arranged by our excellent attendant orderly Ino Ram. It was terribly hot and stuffy and we were dead tired, so thankfully got to bed though it was only 8 p.m.

20th On the Brahmaputra. A peaceful day, spotting alligators of which there are many, and resting, to make up for the last few hard days.

22nd Arrived at Calcutta. Reached Goalundo late last night having been

'Entrance[2] to ancient fort at Dimapur (Cachari)' 1901

'Monolith discovered at Dimapur when tracing line for railway through the Nambhur forest, N.E. Assam - remains of phallic worship - conjectured at 2000 years old'.

delayed by our boat sticking on a sandbank in the river – lost our mail train, but the next was kept for us. There we parted from our faithful Ino Ram who had seen us so far, such a good useful fellow. No agents met us at Sealdah so our luggage arrangements kept us very late and we never reached the Hills house and breakfast till nearly 11 o'clock. Such a warm welcome from dear old Charlie who is looking wonderfully better than when we passed through on our way to Kohima 16 months ago, but Fannie is seedy, and in bed and it is sad to see her looking so ill and frail.

23rd Shopping all morning and business, and a drive in the evening.

---

2.   Over 50 years earlier Browne-Wood described the old fort at Dhemapoor, covered in jungle: 'The gateway is of brick, quite perfect at present, but must very shortly fall to pieces, as huge trees have taken root at the top of it….. there is also a wall of 8 feet high and 4-5 feet deep surrounding the fort'. (Browne-Wood. *Report extract.* 1844).

24th Sunday. Dear old Fannie showed me all her photos and letters from S. Africa – it is so terribly sad. Ms. Brereton and Ms. Beresford came to see me – it is nice to see such old friends. A noble Tiffin basket has been added to our luggage by dear old Charlie to see us on our way.

'Gauhati Dak bungalow' February 1901

'Steamers[3] on the Brahmaputra' Gauhati February 1901

---

3. A steamship service from Calcutta along the Brahmaputra was first set up in 1844 and this was the main means of access to the Naga Hills. The service continued until the Indo-Pakistan conflict of September 1965. (Bhattacharya, *The Brahmaputra*. 2004).

Chapter 8

Kohima and Christmas tour
December 1901

Kohima. Dec 5th 1901

We have been here 12 days now – had an uncomfortable voyage out, found it terribly hot in Bombay in landing on Nov 5th, just a month ago – went up to Cawnpore with Lil on the 6th arriving on 8th, left Mona Gough with her mother and parted from Lil who went on to Umballa. Started for Calcutta next morning, and on the 10th saw dear old Lel's face looking out for me as I came in to Calcutta. Three hot, busy days there, a night journey to Goalundo which we reached on 13th – 3 days on steamer to Gohati, 16th halt, another night journey to Dimapur, reached noon 17th in pouring rain – a hovel of a dak Bungalow to put up in, and started in rain next day in Carts. The road <u>awful</u> after the rain and could only do one stop a day at the rate of from 1 to 2 miles an hour, and finally reached this on 22nd. Encountered a Hamadryad snake below Ghas Pani, which however was too bloated and gorged with food to attack us, a merciful escape. Busy today preparing for our first move to Tesima tomorrow.

6th to 10th at Tesima, the little place looking very pretty, the garden full of roses. Mr. and Mrs. Bliss came out (putting up in a tent) the former's presence officially required for watching the men shooting off their inter-battalion matches. They shot exceedingly well, 60 points better than last year, which is a good advance. The 8th was such a busy day the range could not be left all

'Angami warrior' Kohima

'Guard house. S. end of Khonoma fort'

day so breakfast was taken out there. Bitterly cold in the afternoon with a high wind.

10th returned to Kohima. Seedy, Blisses came in after Tennis.

11th Miserable with neuralgia – not much doing all day. Capt. Kennedy came to breakfast before starting for Dimapur. Sent him one little Xmas present, Burmese silver sweet dishes – very pleased with them.

12th. Bitter. Blisses and 3 Subalterns came up in the evening. Mr. Grant back from Shillong – beaming! Mr. White from camp at Maiankong, order up to our Battalion to go on up to Tank for this Waziristan blockade. Knows the Biddulphs and Martins well – stays at Overbury – had lots to say about the family. Young Eardley Wilmot much interested in Lel's Naga curios.

13th Out to Khonoma – the cold wind brought back neuralgia.

14th Very miserable all day.

15th Better but not up to going on with Lel to Paplongmai so returned to Kohima.

16th Came out to Tesima to finish sketches etc. and stayed 17th and 18th.

19th got up with the dawn and packed up. Started about ¼ to 8 a.m. and rode in to Kohima getting in a little before 9. A lovely morning – hard frost. Lel very fit, got back from Paplongmai last night.

20th Tennis, had some fair sets. Blisses came in and discussed plans. Mr. Daniell, and young Eardley Wilmot dined.

21st Lel and I went down and had a strum on the Kerr's piano, such a nice one. Lel much taken with "Violets" by E. Wright.

22nd Ghenna up in Kohima village, but not nearly so good as last year. Tomorrow will be their best day – very busy preparing for tomorrow's start. Home mail, and nice letters from Wyn and Aunt Madge and Toosie. Such a capital report of Wyn, by last mail, dear little fellow.

'Kohima, Nagas dancing on parade ground'

23rd. Got off this morning in very good time the Blisses appearing at our house soon after 11 a.m. – very busy before starting getting little Arthur Bagley's presents ready for him, which I hope will make his Xmas day happier. A lovely morning, not too hot. Halted for a little Tea and bread and butter (Mrs. B. and I) while the 2 husbands went on, when Mrs. B. astonished both herself and me by fainting! but was soon all right again. Got here about 3.30 found our camp set out much as it was this day last year down in the Zulu valley. This time we have 12 sepoys and 2 N.C.O.s, Wazira one of our friends on the Sema trip and the faithful Ino Ram among them.

'Angami in gala attire', Kohima

24th A hard frost this morning and very cold before starting. Got off about 10 a.m. Mrs. B. and I riding and going in the "Topper" most of the way till we reached the descent to the Tisoo, the Zulu valley being 2,780 and the Tisoo 2,700 – as on this day last year, very hot and trying. A pleasant rest and breakfast on the banks of the river, and L. photo'd the scene and then that dreadful climb up from the river of 2000 odd ft. The hill had all been jhoomed and cleared of trees since last year and there was no shade and Mrs. B, whom the Topper affected with sickness, and was afraid of the pony, got a bit knocked up. However we got in all right about 4.30 p.m. and Tea pulled us together and here we are camped again in <u>Kekrima</u> in the same spot as last year. Made a couple of little sketches of these wonderful horned houses. The Zulu and the Siju meet about 15 miles down and form the Doyang, which eventually empties into the Dunseri in the Nambur.

'Kekrima, 24.12.01'

25th Xmas Day, but not much to mark it beyond pretty cards for all of us which the Tolleys had kindly sent out for us by the Guard. We had hoped to start early as our march was to be a long one, but were delayed by Mrs. B. being seedy somewhat. However we got off at last, rather late, had a long march along the sunny face of the Kopermetso Range, halted for breakfast at a pretty spot where were some ghenna stones, with the usual sort of stone shelf for resting, which the Nagas make, very convenient but blazing hot which somewhat marred the comfort of the meal and the rest. Then up a sort of staircase through the forest, self riding, Mrs. B. in Topper over the top of the Range, the Pass being 7,600ft., then dropped down incessantly on the reverse and shady side through deep forest where it was almost dark in places. I got desperately tired at last, not being very fit, so got into the Topper, and the men carried me cleverly and with great care through desperately thick jungle where was hardly room to get along, then uphill, when we came out again into light, and finally over a shoulder when I came up with the rest of the party who had gone on. Our object had been to reach <u>Razema,</u> but it was already 4 p.m. and we were still some miles distant, so we decided to content ourselves with halting the night at <u>Charboma</u>, E. 6,600 a little village which lay on the slope just below us. Our tents, with all the other baggage, had gone on but were soon recalled, and pitched on a grassy plat to the north of the village.

'Chaboma 25.12.01'

Meantime we got Tea ready and set out in the verandah of one of ten houses where we also sheltered our shivering forms from the bitter cold wind. I think I have seldom felt more sick, tired, than I did that day and through the last $\frac{1}{2}$ of the march could have laid down and never cared a straw what became of me! Our night at Kekrima was not a success exactly, very disturbed, talkative people, barking dogs and cocks who loudly saluted the coming dawn every half hour through the night so we had had little sleep before our start.

'Razema 26.12.01'

26th <u>Razema</u>. Got off from Charboma before breakfast, still feeling very seedy, so got carried most of the way. Most beautiful views of Forest covered mountains, and spurs of wonderful terraced cultivation running down in a <u>deep</u> valley, Razema standing on a little hill projecting out into this valley, with high bluffs above it, and beautiful golden coloured open slopes below them. Curious little clay figures of Nagas, Sepoys and animals were hanging in the verandah of the house where our kitchen was located. Here we are quite close to the Manipur frontier. The Razium runs at the bottom of the valley, below this and forms the boundary. The view is wonderful, Sarametti appearing quite comparatively near, that unknown splendid mass of mountain, and Ketzatoolaso Rock, a sharp and prominent peak to the South of Sarametti in Manipur territory. Our approach to Razema was most picturesque, our train of Naga headmen in their red cloths, and others brightly attired winding along behind us on the shady narrow path, then as we entered the village all its occupants were gathered in groups, and up on their high platforms, eagerly on the look-out for us, and full of intense curiosity and interest.

'Halt by the way on road between Razema and Thetchilumi'

27th Thetchilumi.[1] E 6,200. We got off from Razema in good time – so cold, hard frost when we first got up. A long, and very steep downhill took us into the Chaboma valley, and from there we started on the most trying ascent I have ever known, the sun blazing, the path as near perpendicular as possible up a hillside covered with deep heavy grass, its heavy swathes just the height of my face, almost suffocating me as I struggled up. It had to be done on foot for some distance as the path was a mere ledge on the face of the hill, and I thought I should drop! but L. gave me a hand and dragged me on till we got to where the path improved a bit, and then I got into my "Topper". Oh! Blessed

---

1. Some 15 years earlier three men from Khonoma were killed while trading in Manipur. In retaliation a large force attacked the village of Shipvomi. The D.C. of the Naga Hills decided (mistakenly) this was the work of Thetchulomi which was burned in punishment. (Reid, *History*. 1942).

Kohima and Christmas Tour – December 1901 | 177

'Thetchilumi' December 1901

relief! but my poor bearers had a stiff time I fear, while my right arm also got quite stiff and tired pushing aside the heavy grass which impeded our ascent. Now and then at last we got some bits of level, or descent, which we hailed joyfully, and L. got some capital orchids, *Vanda Parishii* and *Renanthera*, and finally about 1 p.m. our eyes and spirits were cheered by the sight of breakfast preparing for us in the most lovely shady stream bed; cool, deep shade, ferns of every description, palm trees, and the Jheam[?] tumbling along through its rocky bed. How glad we were to halt, rest and refresh ourselves, breakfast making new beings of us – then a little stroll down stream to let the coolies get on while L. shewed us a lovely waterfall he had discovered, and then on again up another fearsome hill. But at the top how exquisite the view, the sun shining on the golden grass of the hill we had just passed over, the trees gorgeous in the richest of autumn tints and the shadows and distances of the deepest and most intense blue. One more steep descent, into the Thetchilumi valley, and then one last long steep ascent up to the village. We found the men wondering where to put the tents, and it was very cold waiting about, but presently we were summoned by L. to the top of the village where we found a nice, clean space and soon the tents were up, and Tea, that blessed meal, made its comforting appearance before long. It was a long day though, as we did not get in till nearly 5 p.m. It is not at all a well-to-do looking village; it is large, but the people look poor, ill-fed, and careless of their appearance.

'Thetchilumi 27.12.01'

The view from up here is grand, the village standing on a spur overlooking Sarametti and all the country in between. From here you see the position of the new Kuki villages of Ishan, which a few years ago did not exist. Now the Kukis are a powerful people about there, and are harrying their Naga neighbours grievously – evidence in itself which shows how the tribe is steadily pushing northwards.

28th Purbami. E. 5,600 Thank goodness an easier march than yesterday! though bits of this were fairly bad too, but we made a good start and got in here soon after 4 p.m. not bad going for 12 such miles. Our start was, as usual, a long steep descent for about an hour, then continuous sort of tightrope walking along the divisions between the rice khets, most beautiful terracing it was, till we came to a stream, then one of those fearsome ascents for a short while after which a pleasant gradual ascent up to Kezabama, our half way halt for breakfast. Our coolies were to be changed here, and such an eager, expectant crowd met us, full of curiosity, never having seen any white women before, and all so cheery and anxious to take up our loads. Breakfast was soon set in the verandah of one of the houses.

'Corner in Kezabama Eastern Angami 28.12.01'

A curious and admiring crowd gathered all round, while the lady of the house where we were sitting (such a nice looking woman) and her husband, an elderly well-mannered savage dressed in an extraordinary cloth, kept nearest to us, and ventured on closer inspection than the others. I showed them my watch, and telescope pencil the working of which elicited murmurs of wonder; my gloves also were marvels, but much more still were my <u>hands</u> when I drew my gloves off! The woman felt them and turned them over, comparing them with her own, with many exclamations, and when I undid my cuff and turned up my sleeve showing my arm, the wonder and exclamations increased, as they saw its colour and felt its texture! They were greatly interested in our food, of which we gave them little samples, bread, or butter, both of which they disliked, while biscuit, treacle and sugar they approved. It is a smart flourishing looking village, the people a fine lot, cheerful and well to do. I was quite sorry to leave them, but time was precious and on we had to go, down hill first, then past Yasabasni, whose red clothed goanbura came out to greet us with his generous little offering of eggs, and from there on our path was of the roughest, a good deal of it at intervals down steep rocky watercourses, or along more level ones, or along the narrowest of mud banks where a false step either landed you in a stream one side or let you down towards unfathomed depths hidden by undergrowth on the other, as we made our way up towards the head of

'Kezabama' December 1901

this great valley. We were on the shady side of the valley now, our path way overhung by forest growth which made it very dark, while a chilly breeze had sprung up making it very cold, making it really appear as if late evening were setting in and we still had some little way to go so that it seemed curious presently, having crossed the valley and begun to mount the other side, to find ourselves suddenly coming out into bright daylight and sun again and that the time was not yet 4 p.m! One more final steep ascent accomplished by me in the blessed Topper landed us at last in Purbami. As to these same ascents and descents, they are all generally of about 2000ft. which is quite enough at one time. It is a very picturesque village, built on a steep slope, its centre street with its line of huge horned houses and scenes of Naga native life a most perfect picture in its way. Along our road we have passed quantities of wild apple trees, the fruit a good size, a fine colour, flavour good also, but very sour; also fig trees loaded with fruit which will be ripe in 2 or 3 months; also rubber trees, yews also and willows. The Ghenna stones of this region are quite marvelous in size, larger than any I have seen elsewhere, some of them quite 20ft. high.

'Purbami' December 1901

The view up the Messidajuma valley was grand, such steep cliffs falling abruptly down into its narrow depth. Our poor Sibboo, the cook, has fallen ill with a bad eye, very painful, quite unable to work, so all responsibility falls on the faithful Asimoo, a little hard but he gets through it, including the bread making, and considering the alarming appetites which our party contains it is wonderful how he manages. The pony also has gone sick with a lump on his back, which I fear will take a long time curing – dear, cat-like little beast! it is a pity.

'Purbami' December 1901

29th Chadoma. E. 6,500. Got off rather later this morning though we had got up earlier. Uphill first, through deep forest in which we got some orchids and nice asparagus plants, crossing the Kopermetzo at 7700ft. From the top was a grand Panorama looking back which L. and I stopped for some time to admire; 7 ranges of mountains with Sarametti standing out against the skyline, and for the first time, the sky being so clear and our position so unusually high we caught a glimpse of three distant peaks beyond Sarametti, which must undoubtedly be in Burma. Beyond the 3rd range on which stands Lozaphehemi the village on the extreme East of the Angami country, we overlooked the valley of the Lanyar, one of the eastern boundaries where it joins the Tuzu which flows on ultimately into the Chindwin. This range of the Kopermetzo forms the watershed between the Brahmaputra and the Irrawaddy, and now having left the country which feeds the latter in which we have spent the last few days, we are back once more in the old country of the former. It was a short march, but being done in one spell without breakfast on the way in, consequence of there being no water, it was a bit tiring. We did not get in till after 2 p.m. which seemed an unduly late hour for some famished appetites to wait for their meal.

This village was punished in '77 first for raiding when there was some fighting here, and again in '79 and 80 for joining in the Khonoma rising. We have just been for an evening stroll into the village and given intense pleasure by watching and assisting a busy old woman who was setting up her loom. Mrs. Bliss and L. helped her in the unwinding of her thread, and she being apparently a bit of a wag her remarks every now and then convulsed the company around. I suppose this occasion of an English woman having come to assist at this work will be talked of for months, perhaps years! The clouds have come down and it is dark and cold and looks like rain.

'Chadoma'

30th <u>Zulu Valley</u>. A very late start as the coolies could not be collected quickly, but I don't think we regretted the extra leisure, our night having been a very disturbed one, groups of Nagas who had apparently been dining out returning at odd hours singing their quaint choruses as they passed along, extremely pretty and musical but a little ill-timed as regarded our desires for sleep. The cocks also, like those of Kekrima, were persistently anticipating the dawn all through the night in a most distracting manner. Also arose some commotion about 1 p.m. over the arrival of our daks, sent out by 2 sepoys to meet us. Such a budget, as it proved this morning, but rather a blank for me as there was nothing from or about Wyn.

'Angami Naga house in Chadoma village a grave to the right and a woman arranging her threads prior to weaving in front of house'

I got a little sketch of some graves while waiting for the start, rather different from others I have seen. A curious little custom connected with the funeral ceremonies of these Angami warriors is that when one such dies by a natural death and not in warfare, the nearest male relative wounds the head with a spear thrust so that he may appear to the authorities of the other world to have died fighting. The morning was gloriously clear and the view of the whole Barail range and all the country round perfect. We got off about 10 a.m. starting of course with a steep descent – down at the bottom was a stream to be crossed by a little bridge of one plank. It was curious to see all the coolies as they came to it doing their little "pooja" bit, each gathering a handful grass as he came up to it and laying it down in front of the bridge to which each then made a little reverence as he passed on. Then we came to a river winding among rice fields and eventually turning into a deep, narrow rocky valley. It had to be crossed 5 times so I negotiated this part in my "Topper". Then the path, a mere narrow track turned up high on the right bank eventually coming out on the Govt. path leading to Cheswajuma and the Sema country. Here Lel joined me, (and we had got far ahead of the others) and we made our way down to the Siju bridge and there on its shingle bank we started breakfast going, while I showed the coolies how to make "Ducks and Drakes" which they were quick at picking up. Breakfast over, began the climb up. Lel and Mr. B. went on ahead while Mrs. B. and I followed with our "Toppers", quite indispensible as the Coolies insisted on going all the perpendicular short cuts, which I had no intention of doing on foot. We came to one very long and very steep stretch starting on which my smart young Naga (such a nice looking team of 3 I had this time) took me up, and putting all his power into it went off, shouting and grunting and bursting through all the thick grass like a rampant young buffalo, without check or halt, laughed at and cheered by the others up to the top where he set me down with a flourish and a final shout of triumph alongside Lel and Mr. B. who were sitting there. It really was a splendid performance and done with such goodwill, cheeriness and fun; they are a delightful people. From there it was a short and easy descent to this where now for the 4th time we have got our camp. The sepoys have sheltered themselves in little "lean-tos" of boughs and grass but the Nagas have a most ingenious and simple sort of shelter of their own – they take the tops of the tall grass in a line, bend them over and tie them down half way up the opposite line of grass, and then cut more grass and spread it above like a thatch, and at once they have got a warm, sheltered little burrow in which to lie down and sleep. Having heard them singing last night at Chadoma, we told Lohoki the dobasha we should like them to sing for us this evening so after dinner a party of 8 came up and stood by the fire in a ring and sang those soft, quaint antiphonal sort of chants of theirs (4 to each group), <u>most</u> musical, such beautiful chords, and all in a sort of minor strain. They sang several changes of chants and I think were pleased at our evident appreciation of their performances.

'Below Chadoma' December 1901

31st Kohima. Breakfasted at the little Naga rest house about 4 miles out and got in about 3 p.m. Had a new pony to ride this march, rather untrained, but nice enough once you are on its back. And so ends our Xmas tour. And as regards food we got back only just in time, for such were the appetites that had to be supplied that though I thought I had taken an ample margin of everything, our last breakfast on the road saw the final clearing out of the last bit of bread, last biscuit, last bit of butter, jam, everything in fact! The supplies had only just held out. – We went up to Tennis later and I asked solitary young Daniell to come in to dinner. Poor fellow he sat so late chatting with Lel that after the long day's outing I am afraid I most palpably snoozed often before 11 p.m. when he left.

'Bridge over Sijoo River EL. 2400'

CMS, Captain and Mrs. Bliss

Kohima and Christmas Tour – *December 1901*

'Naga Rest House near Kohima 1901'

'Near Kohima 31.12.01'

Chapter 9

Kohima
January 1902

Jan 1st 1902. Parade and Feu-de-Joi at 9 a.m.

4th Trial of Teams for 44th Sports which Lel had to go and judge on their Parade Ground. Old Rajobin won the Single stick. Bitterly cold, and all glad when it was over, the ladies to turn in to tea with Miss Kerr and the men to go off to the Mess. Lel followed and joined me as I walked home. The Willmores (Dr.) Capt. K. and Mr. Daniell and Mr. Pritchard dined.

5th Sunday.

6th Made an experiment of wild apple jelly; not quite a success in flavour. Went out to find Lel as he was late, found him at the Tolleys. Heard a new Assistant Surgeon is coming, a native, with a Scotch wife, and the Willmores must turn out to make room for him.

7th Sports for the 44th and N.H.M.P. Our men easy first in the khud race, a very trying course. Karti Ram, N.H.M.P. first in the native officers' race. Our team nowhere in the tug-of-war. Major Kerr asked me to give away the prizes, and it was rather an amusing business.

8th Lel very cheap, bad head and cold. Saw Mr. Melvill, Inspector of Signaling, arrive as I went out and found L. at the Tolleys. Tolley[1] much excited over the Signaling, which he has been training his men at most assiduously.

'Phaius Wallichii'

9th Went with Mrs. Tolley[2] to call on all the wives of the native officers, an undertaking which took me 2½ hours to get through. It was interesting and amusing. Mrs. Jamaluddin is a Naga, a nice, pleasant looking woman, and could speak Hindustani fairly so we got on all right, in fact I was quite astonished to find out how much I could talk when actually obliged to! Quite a large spread was brought in for our entertainment, a tray for each containing Tea in a large cup (very sweet and with lots of milk), sweetmeats, nuts, raisins and biscuits and jam. Of these we partook as much as we could, and I showed the lady and Mrs. Ziaram who had joined us Wyn's photos which I had brought with me. They knew about him

Wyn, in cadet uniform at school in England

---

1.   In the N.H.M.P. a European Sergeant Major looked after recruits, did a certain amount of drill and also helped out a little as Quartermaster. LWS writes of the Sergeant Major when he first took up his post; 'a first rate drill sergeant, but his thirsty nature and the vehemence with which he quarrelled led to my having to get rid of him'. He thought Tolley a first rate man and clearly got on with him well. Some 18 months after LWS' departure Sergeant Tolley was sat at dinner in his house when he was shot dead through the window, the round narrowly missing his wife. An 18 year old bugler, Sudai Ram, to whom Tolley had awarded three days drill for being improperly dressed on parade, was the apparent murderer – he shot himself shortly afterwards. Tolley was described as a strict disciplinarian and there was some doubt that Sudai Ram acted alone. (LWS, *Memoir.* 1926; Monahan, *Letter.* 1904).

2.   '… and we got up to Kohima in time for General Macgregor's inspection of the 44th G.R. and N.H.M.P. The general was a huge man with a magnificent waist, and the dignity of the proceedings was somewhat upset by Sergeant Tolley's little son who with his mother was standing near the saluting post looking on. The little chap went a bit forward, and looking up with awe at the huge figure on an equally huge horse, piped out clearly to be heard by all, just as the general salute finished, 'Mummy, he's got an awful big tummy'. Whereat the great man glared down and said 'Madam, have the goodness to take away that d-d little mass of truth'. (LWS, *Memoir.* 1926).

from hearsay and were much interested, and I was touched by the sympathetic way in which they spoke of the trial it must be for mother and son to be so long and so far apart. "The heart cannot be happy so," they said, which is very true. When we rose to go Mrs. J. took my hand and drew me away into her own private room and there showed me two pretty Kohima cloths. "These," she said, "are the clothes my people wear, and I want to give them to you" and therewith handed them to me along with a pretty red silk handkerchief from Manipur. She did it all so prettily and kindly and then said she would not trouble me with carrying them but would send them to my house for me later, which she duly did. From her we went to Mrs. Rajobin, a Gharwali and very pretty woman with 3 boy babies more or less and 2 little step daughters older, very pretty children.

'44th G.R. lines from our garden'

They also looked at Wyn's photo and talked about it with interest, and all the children were made to salute it as their mother held it up. Here we also ate sweets and drank Tea. And so it was the same with all, with Mrs. Diaram another very pretty woman, also a Gharwali, with a very pretty little daughter, and two babies. Mrs. Belbong no. 2 a more homely looking woman and Mrs. B. no. 1 who kept rather in the background; at all these places we had to eat oranges and were offered cigarettes which we took but did not smoke. All went swimmingly till we came to Mrs. Sonjai, a pure Gurkhin, big, solid

LWS

and moonfaced like her worthy husband and she could neither speak nor understand a word of anything but her own language. Here indeed we were at a deadlock! in spite of Herkia's (our attendant orderly who speaks English) attempts at interpreting. She stood, so we also stood and after making signs and trying to speak and getting no further with it, we presently thought we'd better go, so made our adieus and left. Thereon followed sounds of objection and dissatisfaction, and on our asking our interpreter what it was all about, "you have not sat down, she says" was his reply and so back we had to go and <u>sit down</u>, while the lady also squatted on a stool with her little girl in her arms, and we had to begin all over again and eat oranges also into the bargain. However we got off at last and then Wazira the Dogra was the last visit we had to pay. We found him as well as his wife at home, the latter very pretty and most beautifully dressed and ornamented, wonderful silver ornaments all over her head, and gold things in her nose. She talked nicely but was very shy, while Wazira did the honours like a real gentleman. Glasses of milk (warm) were brought us and very nice sweetmeats and while we discussed these, at our request Wazira took his Sitar which stood in the corner and played to us, very pretty, weird music it was. A little more talk and then we left, to find the day had turned dark and cold with a thick driving fog, so I was glad enough to get in. – In the evening the Kerrs, Blisses and Mr. Saunders dined. Mr. Melvill called, had been quartered at Dehra and Chokrata, so knew the 2nd Gurkhas well.

10th A busy day preparing for Lel's going off to camp at Maiankong.³ Lel had to spend his day checking the Signalers. Tremendous rivalry between Tolley and N.H.M.P. and Dorward and his 44th. Lel got in late to breakfast, then office, and then we started for a bike turn but it was too late and the road too bad to enjoy it.

11th Lel started off at 9 a.m. with his men, going strictly on Service scale, no bed and no tent. It is a bit dull and lonely. Went out to sketch on the 44th Parade ground but found it bitterly cold so was pleasantly attracted by Miss Kerr's invite to come in and have some Tea. Dined at Capt. Kennedy's, a cheery evening, all Kohima there, that is 7 in all, of which wonderful to say 4 were ladies!

12th Sent off Lel's parcel, coats, rum etc. Breakfasted with Capt. K. and shall dine there. Very cold and cloudy, working up for rain.

13th Dined with Capt. K., the Tolleys there. Capt. K. told us of some curious customs among the people of the Garo hills, how marriage is there by capture, and it is the man who is captured and carried off, the women being the chief authority in that tribe. The man is sometimes coy and runs away, when he has to be recaptured; sometimes he is unwilling, and runs away and has to be recaptured more than once. If this occurs several times he is eventually given up and someone else is looked out for. All property in this tribe goes in the female line from which also the name of the family is taken. Capt. K. sent down a little monkey for me to keep, a dear little gentle thing, but unfortunately full grown, so I fear will never tame thoroughly. She is the same sort, and comes just in time to replace poor, dear little "Jesmie" who, to my grief, died last night, fell from her perch when the "long" who was near would not let her get up, and so she was strangled. It is grievous to think of the dear little thing having died such a dreadful death. This little thing is so starved it is too weak to sit up, lies down and just swallows bits of orange as I give them.

---

3. 'The 3rd Brahmins were in Manipur then and Col. Lumsden held a camp of experience for his regiment and the 44th G.R. from Kohima at Mayankhong in Feb 1902 which I obtained permission to attend with as many of my men as possible. Collecting some 250 or more we tramped down with the 44th going light and bivouacking, only 3 carts for rations. It lasted a fortnight and was a good camp, many excellent schemes were worked out, the N.H.M.P. were on their mettle to do well with regulars and they did so'. (LWS, *Memoir*. 1926).

'N.H.M.P. orderly room and recruits parade'

16th My Tea Party to all the native officers' wives came off and was most successful. Mrs. Tolley came and was a great help, but the ladies were very late in coming, not appearing till 8, instead of 7 as arranged. I suppose it was not dark enough in their opinion! I had got a lot of little stools for them to sit on, which they preferred to chairs. We gave them scent all round, a little poured in their hands which they spread on their hair, but of the sweetmeats which I had prepared they would take none but a few almonds and raisins; it was not their custom, they said, to eat before strangers, but the little packets of Pan, those they took and ate. Only Mrs. Jamaluddin (who is a Naga) and Mrs. Sunjai who is a Goorkin and can neither speak nor understand anything but her own tongue were absent. All those who came were most beautifully dressed and had all their best ornaments on, very pretty indeed, especially Mrs. Wazira (Dogra), Mrs. Dayaram who brought a very pretty little girl with her, and we showed them photos and curios, Burmese and Naga, and their tongues wagged among each other no end and I played my Guitar to them and I think they enjoyed themselves thoroughly. I took them into my bedroom too, which filled them all with curiosity, and one remarked on Wyn's[4] photo (the 4 year old one) standing on my dressing table, how I had my "Baba" there, always smiling at me, which I thought was very nice – and then with many

---

4. Wyn was their second son, born in 1888 some 18 months after the death of their firstborn, Talbot, who died aged 15 months.

expressions of pleasure they all trooped off, and a little after 9 Mrs. T. and I got our dinner at last!

23rd Had all the station and Mrs. Tolley (9 in all) up to Tea, with band in the garden. Tea was laid out on the end of the dinner table and the Porch turned into a sitting room, looking very nice, and Capt. K's excellent factotum came and waited, my only table servant being little Kulu, Sibboo's boy, about 3ft high! who however has been doing splendidly and whom I made very proud the other day by the present of a new little shirt and Dhoti in which to wait on me. It was a dull afternoon, but the Band played an excellent programme and people were amused strolling about and seeing the animals till it got dark when we sat over the fire.

'Kohima visits Phesama'

27th Mrs. Tolley brought Mrs. Jamaludin to Tea, escorted by her nephew whom we presently sent to fetch the 2 Mrs. Sunjai, on hearing that they were ready and anxious to come also. Mrs. J. and her nephew had no prejudice against eating my sandwiches (they would not eat sweets) and drinking Tea with us, which was pleasant and satisfactory. The others brought 3 children, and the elder wife being able to talk a little Hindustani acted interpreter to the other. Mrs J. is an exceedingly nice woman, such nice manners and talks with such a friendly interest in all one's affairs. I played my Guitar and sang to them and she and her nephew were immediately interested in it, touching and fingering, and praising it after I had set it down. The boys and girl smoked cigarettes, and when they all left, Hira Sing handed the dish of sweets (as on the last occasion) outside, and they took them all off with them. That is their way. A message came from Lel during the party, lamp signaled from Jakoma. So I sent another out, "Entertaining another party of Subadarnis, all going capitally".

25th Dined at the Kerrs.

'N.H.M.P. on parade'

28th Lel came back, he and his men marching in, a mass of dust, about noon, all very fit, in good spirits and grand training after their fortnight odd of daily hard work. Lel went out on strict "Service" scale, no tent, his shelter a basha of twigs, grass and leaves, through which the winds raged and their dogs pranced at will regardless of doors, his bed on the ground from whence he was free at all hours of the night to study astronomy through the gale stripped roof. The cold was intense, heavy frost on the ground up till 9 a.m. but he kept very fit through it all.

29th busied ourselves about the Club garden in which Lel has worked wonders.

31st Tea, Band and Tennis at the Club.

Feb. 1st Dined at Capt. K.'s, that funny old character Surgeon Colonel Cave-Calthrop there, with his epigrams, verses and stories. The last few days those dreadful winds have set in which give no peace or rest indoors or out; they have come very early this year – not due till nearly March.

'Con and the Mirris'

2nd Very busy morning packing for our start on our long tour to Tamlu. Got everything off by about 11 a.m. and then went to breakfast with Capt. K. and finally got off ourselves about 1.30, the dear little "Long" and "Kalu" whining and bemoaning our departure. In spite of the sun it was almost cold as we got further from Kohima and this evening the cold is great, the wind very high again making our chimney smoke to an unbearable extent, necessitating periodical opening of doors which chill one to the bone. <u>Bed</u> is the only bearable place!

3rd Our morning Tea was ushered in by a storm of Mirris! who swamped us and gambled over us with an absolute disregard of human anatomy not altogether unpainful on occasion – the big Mirri, and the lesser Minkali and Mikeh, all solid and weighty, had much to say and a large amount of spirits to let off. Went from a walk round the pools, very cold and the dogs so wild we decided not to bring them out again. The wind furious in the evening and bed again the only place of comfort!

4th Busy writing off letters and gardening. Took a walk with L. in the evening, but so cold we were glad to keep the sheltered side of the hill. Old Sunjai came round the garden with us, and now he has got used to me has quite lost his shyness and chats away quite easily. He is evidently pleased and proud at his ladies having been to Tea with me! and such a select party too, only the Subadar Major's wife besides!

Chapter 10

Tour to Tamlu
February 1902

5ᵗʰ Chichama. Got off about 11.15 and accomplished the usual perpendicular miles at a much slower rate than usual, my coolies with my Topper being the feeblest I have yet come across, to the extent that one even dropped me! a thing that has never happened before. Our entry into the village was heralded by a fanfare from its Cocks, the whole hillside on which the village is built breaking out into a Chorus of crows of every variety of tone, pitch and quality, a most curious effect. The "Mikeh" who we have brought proves most troublesome, irreconcilable to her severance from the Minkaleh, so she is to go back.

6ᵗʰ Themakodima. 13 miles, started about 9.30. Breakfasted on the way and got in about 2.30. These northern Angamis are a very dirty lot, none of the smartness of the Central and Eastern Angamis, perhaps due to the influence of their near neighbours the dirty Semas, whose village of Kemphima we see from the road. It is not a pretty season for marching, the trees and

'Moimang[1] and Io/Ayo, Lengta Nagas, Tamlu' February 1902

---

1. Dress and ornaments denote status and achievement. In this chapter the three photos of Moimang, Io and Wang show them accoutred in their best dress (previously described by Connie on 12ᵗʰ August 1900) which consisted of spears with tufts of goats' hair; hide shields; daos with dyed goats' hair; cane helmets embellished with boars' tusks, hornbill feathers and goats' hair; conch shell ear ornaments; necklets of boar tusks; armlets of ivory; wristlets of cowrie shells; cane and bark belts with tassel at the back; a representative head-taker's basket and a muzzle-loader.

undergrowth all dry and withered, and the views obscured by the smoke of the jhooming which also fills the air with ashes of grass but the temperature is perfect for it.

7th Wokka. Lota Naga. A double march today, breakfasting at Kotsama bungalow, a cool day luckily, but our poor coolies had a long tramp with 2 miles added on to their 13 miles march, having come from Tersephomi.

'Grave Chichama N. Angami Feb 6th 1902'

'Grave of a village notable Temakodima 6 Feb1902'

8th Lungtyan. Sema Naga. Another double march, coolies changing at Koio, 2 miles beyond which we breakfasted in a pretty shady corner, having done 10 miles and having 8 to do. Five miles of this was steady downhill to the Doyang bridge, having crossed which I got into my "Topper", making the pony over to Lel to mount the somewhat stiff 3 miles of rise up to this. My little Lota men carried me splendidly each man going for between ½ to ¾ an hour at a stretch easily. My poor "topper" broke soon after our start up the hill but the clever little men took out daos and cut down a bamboo, split it up and mended it up in no time, using their <u>heads</u> as an object on which to split and bend the Bamboo! This little bungalow which used to be so pretty and bright with flowers is looking sadly neglected under its present Chowkidar.

'Lhota Naga grave', 6 February 1902

'Graves at Themakodima - Rengma Nagas' February 1902

Tour to Tamlu – *February 1902* | ***205***

'Lhota woman weaving'

'Sema warriors'

'Sema Naga in war paint'   'Sema Naga in war paint'

9th Numkum. Aoh Naga, a single march today I am glad to say, mostly uphill to this Olympus of the neighbourhood. We breakfast just before the final long ascent, and timing Sibboo found it took 20 minutes from start to finish to light the fire and produce a nice hot stew and Tea. A very cold wind up here and decidedly chilly. Our friend the great Tumsi from sheer indolence has resigned his office of Dobasha which has been taken up by Bindong's husband and we found him up near the war drum lying out taking a "Sun bath" in strictly correct clothing! Alum Kabi, the Chowkidar came up with his little present of vegetables, and Bindong beaming with a tray of oranges; later on too came up Sepoy Maniraj from the barracks below with a huge haunch of sambhur which shed joy among the establishment generally as there was enough for every one, and some lovely vegetables and milk. Such lettuces I have not seen, just like cabbages. Later we went for a turn in the village, a very fine one it is too. It is curious to note the distinctions of the houses; those of the wealthiest who have been able to feast their friends on mitton have their verandah and filled in with thatch to quite low down, those less wealthy who can only run to pig are only entitled to a short covering of their verandah, while the common herd have none at all. The severed trees, each the centre of its khel (or

'Lhota woman'

parish), on which the "heads" brought home as trophies were displayed, still stand and are cherished though no longer applied to their old ghastly use, yet the remembrance of it is still preserved by a few round pots being hung about them. We came upon Alum Kabi's house most glorified with new thatch, deep verandah roof with wonderful ornaments along and hanging from its ridge pole, and yet more wonderful wooden ornaments all round the entrance representing groups of Toucan feathers. He told us with some pride he had been killing a mitton and this was how he showed the glory of his position in consequence! We had of course to go in and drink Zu which his wife prepared and warmed over the fire as we sat round it – a quaint scene.

10th Mokokchung. Aoh Naga. Another single march. We started walking through Nunkum village accompanied by Alum Kabi who explained to us the meaning of the curious slabs of some darkened wood which had puzzled us much, ranged outside the Moranghur. These latter were originally built as guard houses for their several khels, the young bachelors always living in them and some always being on duty to watch to give notice of the approach of any enemy and to sound the war drum to recall the others from the fields. When one of these married he left the Moranghur and had a house of his own, and on leaving set up one of these curious slabs of wood to signify that he had done his full time of service on guard, and now though the Moranghurs are no longer needed as Guard houses, the old custom is still kept up when a man leaves and gets married.

– Our breakfast wandered on very far ahead today and fainting nature hungered long in vain for it, but we came up with it at last in the avenue a little distance from Oongma, all ready for us, and good old Ino Ram dragged up a fine bundle of thatching grass and gave me a lovely seat with a back against a tree and I discussed it in luxury. Lel prefers sitting in the sun, I don't! We took our way through Oongma village, such a scene of desolation when we last passed through it a little more than a year ago when it had just been burnt down, but now all rebuilt again and flourishing. Such a curious, and pretty scene too we came upon at the upper end of the village; a rather smart house with its verandah enclosed with matting and against these walls was set out a great display of bright coloured cloths, lovely necklaces of cut Carnelians, stones and shells and chains of quaint shaped little copper bells of graduated sizes, while alongside stood a grove of brightly ornamented spears, and people in front were sitting about busy chipping wooden and Bamboo ornaments of sorts. Lel at first did not twig the significance of the enclosed verandah, but I guessed at once and sure enough there inside was a lately departed member of the household in his long basket mounted on poles and covered with the pretty bamboo covering they make, in process of being smoke-dried, the people, the members of the household taking the "departure" very cheerfully and apparently rather pleased and proud over the little stir made by the carrying on of the "treatment" and the bright show made by the display of the poor fellow's property outside, while those at work were making sham representations of his arms and ornaments which would be hung around him when, the process being completed, he would be put away in a little hutch of his own under the avenue of big trees just outside the village. Much did we regret that we had allowed the camera to go on and so could take no photo of the curious scene. It was a much warmer march today and it is pleasant to get in and feel that we need not move tomorrow. Kind old Subadar Major Arjun Rai came up to greet us and later on followed a thoughtful and kindly offering of fowls, fresh eggs and butter, also a lovely basket of vegetables which are a treat.

'Aohs carving a tree trunk'

11th Halted. Very busy writing for English mail, Lel doing his musketry. He invited Mrs. Arjun and the children to come to Tea, which Arjun said they would be very pleased to do and to our amusement when he came up later he said that not only were his wife and children coming but a whole lot of others as well! And duly about 6 p.m. when the flaunting light of day was passed, a great chattering of voices heralded the approach of a whole troop of girls and children, headed by Mrs. Arjun glorious in bright green silk under a black um-

'Aoh Naga grave'

brella. They all trooped in and sat down round the fire, would not drink tea, I found, but liked Ginger bread and cakes, and seemed to enjoy themselves. Mrs. A. is an Angami Naga, a nice mannered woman, but very shy, which latter however was not the case with some of the little Goorkhin wives, who were most chatty and friendly. They spent about ½ an hour with us and then clattered off leaving behind a huge tray of raisins, pistas, walnuts and sugar! Dear old Arjun had been up in the afternoon to bring me a present of 3 fine Tamlu spears, a sash, and wicker helmet.

12th English mail in – Wyn's letter from Bilericay. Busy with some letters. Went to see Mrs. Arjun in her house, and round the married Lines – back again to make a cake before our start tomorrow – then when Lel came in went up to see Mr. Williamson's new house, which is a little beauty.

13th Mongsemdi. Aoh Naga. On the march again today, 15 miles of which I did on foot – a lovely cool day, clouds about with soft sunlights in the distance making beautiful effects. Breakfasted in the corner of the Forest where we took that meal in Aug. 1900. We passed Juju, the road running under and round it for nearly 2 miles. Then Impur, with Chuntia that fine looking village behind slightly to south then Salachu, these all on our left. Further on as we approached this we came in sight of Letam and Nozam quite near but across the border, (the Dikku river) the former having quite lately distinguished itself by making a raid on Chari where it carried off several heads. To accomplish this they had had the impudence to cross the border into our territory making their march all through our land till they came alongside of the unfortunate unsuspecting village just the other side of the river which they thus of course took quite unawares. This offence was represented to the C.C. as deserving of a visitation to Letam and punishment, in which Lel hoped much to have a part, but the C.C. would not have it, a great pity and a great mistake. Closer here are two Mirri villages, Yungundi and Chakpa, who of their own desire have immigrated from the independent country to within our borders for the sake of peace and quietude. This speaks for itself of the vast amount of available and unappropriated land that exists in these hills. A wonderful point in this country is the multitude of different languages which exist among the tribes who inhabit it. All a kindred looking people, supposed to be of kindred origin, and living under very similar conditions and customs, yet speaking an innumerable number of different languages, both within our territory and in the Independent country. Two curious cases are those of the villages of Chungti and Asaringa, offshoots of the Chankong group in the Yungnu valley (in the Independent country) who have migrated far into our territory, many many years ago, Asaringa almost overlooking the plains even, yet still they keep up their distinction from the people they live over, preserving in their distant isolation from it the language and customs of their own tribe. We took a little stroll in the village but it is a miserable looking uninteresting one, has suffered much from big fires and has not recovered.

'Street in an Aoh Naga village'

14th Santong. Passed through Susu – paid a visit to our old friend Panchung Lamba and arranged a deal for cloths on our return. Breakfasted in the old spot outside Oongru with a crowd of admiring spectators. Further on went through Akoya village which we had not visited before and took some photos but the sky was cloudy and light uncertain. Nearly lost our way coming out of this village but found it again at last after a little delay. Saw a quantity of fine

'An Aoh Naga'

orchids which we mean to get on our return. A hotter day, found the march tiring though not a long one.

15th Tamlu, a double march today, breakfasting ½ way at Merongkong, old Lanu the Dobasha coming to meet us with change of coolies. The country looking dreary to a degree with the intensive jhooming which has been going on, whole hillsides for miles, absolutely bare and ready for grain sowing. In one or two places the fires were still going on with a roaring that made itself heard from a tremendous distance, the bamboos bursting with a report like guns, and the smoke towering up in masses of columns that completely shut out all view. One valley brought Sodom and Gomorrah to ones mind in a most lively way. Saw a quantity more good orchids, which must be got. Got in about 5, very tired, Daukam meeting us to escort us.

'Tamlu 16.2.02' Morang

'Tamlu village'

16th Halted. Took sketches, photos of Fort and new Parade ground, wrote letters for mail, and developed photos in evening. The great Io came to see me.

17th Halted. We were to have gone to Namsung a very interesting village about 5 miles off but they've got cholera there, so we gave it up. This evening we have been for a turn in the village, especially to see the Burial tree which stands near the further end of it.

'Daupan and his heads'

'Skulls & children's bodies in the burial tree. Bodies are first smoke dried & afterwards the head is wrenched off & placed in an earthen pot or basket & laid at the foot of tree while the body is wrapped round with leaves of the 'tokapat' pahu & hung up in the fire'.

This village is an offshoot from Bortablung on the other side of the Dikku and brought its trans-Dikku customs with it. Their dead having been smoke dried were packed in canoe shaped coffins, the trunks of trees roughly hollowed and fashioned, covered with a thatch of leaves etc. and placed up in the branches of some selected tree, generally a fine, large one, while the <u>head</u> having been broken off was placed at the foot of the tree in a hollowed block of sandstone, its opening being closed up by a stone fixed in the ground tight against it. These latter we found in quantities all round the base of this tree, a very fine Rubber, while two small coffins still hung in the branches. It was too late to take a photo, and that must be done tomorrow before starting. A little further up the hill we stopped again for me to get the sketch of a house of Bortablung architecture, all these tribes differing in the lines on which they build their houses. "Wang" the "mistri" of the village met us with two fish, just caught from the Dikku, which he presented to us, and then we went on, coming finally, over the top of the hill to a pretty little covered gateway which led into the present Cemetery of this side of the village. Here also one coffin was up in a tree, but the rest were placed on little stands of Bamboo alongside the pathway. The wooden coffins were so curious in shape we said we <u>must</u> take a time exposure photo: but how to manage it! A little looking about brought to light a 3 pronged log, and setting this up with my umbrella as another leg and my coat as a cushion on which to place the Camera case as table, we had an excellent stand and the photo came off; may it only prove good. On our way back we fell in with Io, who begged us to come to his house and see his wife. What a character the man is! he presently took my hand, holding and pressing it, and so conducted me to his house with much state and courtesy. A neat, tidy little house, and Impi looking very well, fat and beaming – he evidently takes great care of her. Then home with Io escorting us, to find Moimang (Dobasha) and "Wang" already there, the latter, nice man, refusing to be paid for his fish which he said was a present, and all 3 made happy with a cheroot and tot of rum apiece. All are to come tomorrow morning in finest attire to have their portraits taken. (Io, however having evidently a great love of finery came up the last thing at night as we were retiring to rest, to show himself off, already dressed in all his finery and war paint, very pleased and talkative, and had to be gently but firmly dismissed, with a cheroot to qualify the dismissal and an explanation that <u>tomorrow</u> was the time when his presence would be wanted!)

18th Our party of "warriors" duly turned up to be photo'd and were very amusing. Having stood for their pictures they presently came up to me, Moimang posturing and posing with his spear, demanding opium (all good humouredly and in fun) or if I could not give the opium,[2] some money to buy it, and then they would dance for me. So I promised them the latter and the two M. and Io began their dance with funny little shouts, ferocious gestures, and spearings of imaginary foes. The D. babu of the place was there, keenly interested in the photographing and anxious for his own picture to be taken. Poor fellow, he is evidently pursuing art under great difficulties with a cardboard box as camera with a little lens stuck in one side. His zeal came out most fervidly on seeing L.'s camera and films of Angami Nagas in Ghenna dress. "Sir I will bring my pop and print some if you will allow", "my pop has two formulas for printing etc. etc." and much more eager talk in which "my pop" figured largely, somewhat enigmatical at first but all right when one understood presently that "my pop" was the P.O.P. paper he used for printing! It is wonderful though what

---

2.   The DC report for 1901-1902 describes the people of Tamlu as being 'confirmed opium-eaters' repeating a remark in the *Census of India* of ten years earlier which claimed the same. In his book earlier Butler discussed opium, giving 1794 as the date it was first introduced into Assam from Bengal. He wrote that two-thirds of the population were addicted and opium was being sold to the people by the government, with a deleterious effect. (Allen, *Naga Hills*. 1905: Butler, *Travels and Adventures*. 1855: Davis, *Census*. 1891).

he continues to do with such poor means; he brought us up to show us, some most excellent prints from L.'s films. At last we got off, a very late start, for bidding farewell to the many interesting folk here, as also to Jemadar Bakshi in command of the Detachment, who has been most kind and attentive to us, took time. Io in all his glory, with many protestations of devotion announced his intention of accompanying us on our way, and walked proudly in front. On his back he had a pretty basket slung, with 4 quaint representations of heads,

'Skulls at foot of tree' Tamlu, February 1902

carved in wood fastened on it, and on our inquiring concerning them he proudly replied that, yes, they represented the heads he had himself taken and proceeded to recount how, but his language is difficult to understand and we could not well follow. The basket is a copy of the veritable article in which they carry off the heads when taken and is more or less part of their "war paint", ready for occasion. – A custom which has a very unsightly effect on the people of this place is the blackening of teeth which all do on attaining to maturity, a fearful disfigurement to our eyes, but accounted an adornment by them. – We passed through <u>Kanching</u> and a little further on halted to cut down a withered tree on which were some beautiful plants of orchids which could not otherwise be reached. For this purpose we had brought along with us 6 sepoys with axes. Seeing it was likely to be a long business I decided to ride on and so farewell had to be said to Io.

'Wuang a Lengta Naga of Tamlu', February 1902

'Moimang, Tablungias,[3] Daupan' and Io

'Tamlu morang upper Khel'

---

3.   Denotes a villager from Tablung, one of the Trans-Dikhu villages. (Woodthorpe, *Letter.* 1876).

It was quite touching. He explained how, having his photo I should go into many countries but could always look at this and say "this is Io" – he expressed his regret in many quaint little ways, and then finally laying one hand on my shoulder, and the other on my chest, with this sort of embrace he turned away, and we went our several ways. Under <u>Meronkong</u> I found Lanu with a large collection of villagers and a change of coolies, and breakfast ready through which I was only half way when L. came up and joined me, with a fine basket of orchids. Breakfast over we started on with Lanu accompanying us, till about 2 miles out at a pretty wayside rest house he said he must return, so we halted and photo'd the scene, a very pretty one, with Lanu in the foreground. At last we made Santong about 5 p.m. a long but not very tiring march. The little Mirri pup we took from here on our way out, a miserable little mass of bones which had been plucked of all its hair and would certainly have soon died, we have brought back quite a jolly little beast, but still timid, the result of former ill-usage.

19th **Mongsendi**. Not so long a march as yesterday's but much more tiring somehow, very late too in getting in, having delayed a good deal on the way. We began by going through Akoya, halting to get the lovely orchids we had noted on our way out, and taking a photo of the village also. Breakfast outside Oongru where Panchung Lambar and other headmen met us anxious to deal in various ornaments. Then through Oongru where passing through the village we saw various unhappy little girls sitting outside their houses enduring the miseries of having been lately tattooed, their poor little legs with the new criss-cross pattern on them looking very sore and swollen, as also their lower lips and chins, the Aoh girls all having 3 lines tattooed from under lip down the chin. Thence on to <u>Susu</u>, Panchung Lambar and others accompanying us, and there we had to visit the former in his house to make a deal for a cloth we wanted. We found the whole village on the stir, preparing for a fete and dance which was to take place tonight, all the ornaments, feathers, necklaces, bright cloths etc. spread out over the platforms at the back of the houses, men and women busy repairing any defects, and the latter smartening up their persons, getting clean faces and smooth hair. The fete is probably in connection with the Sowing which is just beginning. Got in here late and very tired. Lel as usual unflagging has been to the old Stockade and brought back a magnificent orchid.

'Morang in Kanching'

'Lanoo our dobasha from Merangkong and coolies en route to Santong'

20ᵗʰ Mokokchung. Made an earlier start than usual and got in by 4 p.m. Breakfasted in the old place by the bridge in the forest, and got a lot more orchids by the way and a wonderful sort of monstrous moss of which we found one bunch in a tree. Old Arjun kindly as ever, with his present of little comforts.

21ˢᵗ Halt. Took photos of Parade and Fort. Also group of officers outside Fort and on bridge. Went to see Mrs. Arjun. Walked around "Lady's mile" in evening, lovely sunset views, most peaceful.

22ⁿᵈ Halt. A raging wind and clouds piling up. Went and took photos of the Arjun family in the p.m. Later L. and I took a turn down the plains road, then up and round the Lady's Mile. Heavy storms in distance, and rain came up. Old Arjun came in for a smoke and chat.

23ʳᵈ. Made a late start for Nunkum, taking Oongma on the way. Stopped to photo and sketch the big Morunghur. These villages team with children and pigs! If I could only draw them! the former such quaint little figures and the latter so extraordinary with their low, hollow backs, and tummies dragging along the ground, till one wonders they do not wear through into holes! Got in here fairly early and went for a stroll, while Tea was preparing, down the rocky path leading to the village "Anahs"[?], or fields. So wonderfully pretty, the moss covered rocks with the Rhododendrons coming into blossom alongside. Just below this path, in a hollow, are three large blocks of stone which the people here reverence greatly, and from which they trace their origin. The name of the place also is due to this belief, being properly "Lungkum", i.e. Lung, stone – and Kum, birth. On our way up through the village we photo'd the scene and funeral display outside a house where a defunct inmate was being smoked. Further up we came upon a funny scene, the girls and women of one khel all singing. This we were told was part of the punishment meted out to a young man of the khel who had misbehaved; he had to entertain all the women, pay them for singing, and pay them also a fine of rice, which we saw being measured out among them. Yanipong, a village belle, was there and took us into her house and gave us zu, such a pretty smart girl, and her house so nice and clean. The little houris of the place have been buzzing around trying to deal in eggs and cloths and carvings, in which we have made small purchases. Tumsi has also been up with his boy, the former regaled with cheroot and rum, the latter with gingerbread. Just below here is the village of Mangmatung, a fine village spread out along a wide topped low ridge, with a magnificent avenue 1½ mile long leading up to it, of bamboos and trees, the latter increasing in size as they approach the village.

'Group of NHMP officers at entrance to Mokokchung fort' February 1902

'Subedar Arjun Rai and family' February 1902

Tour to Tamlu – *February 1902* | *223*

'Ungma village'

'A death in the house', Nankam

24th Lungtyan. (Sema). Began our day by taking Bindong's photo, in all her best. An uninteresting road, and somewhat hot, all down hill. Found a quantity of orchids, one new one among them. Breakfasted under <u>Mongrung</u>, also Sema, like this. It is curious to think how 14 years ago this was all independent and savage country, these villages often requiring little expeditions against them to keep their savagery within bounds. Got in soon after 2 p.m. and manage to catch one or two butterflies and beetles.

25th Wokka. (Lota Naga). A double march today and rather tiring. I started off ahead of Lel and made my way very quickly down to the Doyang bridge hoping to get some butterflies, but found none. There I left the pony and negotiated the 7 miles uphill chiefly in my "Topper" feeling rather cheap and not disposed for much walking. The hillsides are terribly bare and unsightly, being jhoomed and stripped and tidied up ready for sowing the next crop. Lel walking caught me up before Koio where we breakfasted. There the smiling headman met us and recalled my butterfly catching of former visits. The rest of the way I accomplished mostly on the pony and was very thankful when we got in about 5 p.m.

'The bathing pool at Wokha'

26th Halted. Lel rather bothered over his detachment of Dogras who have been giving trouble. Pompa Sing the new Dep. Coll. came up and sent presents of duck, fowl and oranges. A treat to get milk again. Walked down to the "Lake" which Pompa Sing has cleaned and tidied up, photo'd it and him and came home round the "Lady's Mile".

27th Temakodima. (Rengma). A double march again but on the whole less tiring. I started ahead, Lel having to thrash out various troublesome matters with his Havildar, Tulsi, the Hospital Babu and the Road D.O., his men having given trouble all round. Quantities of violets all along the banks, blue, and white also, the ground in places quite coloured by them, very pretty, but no scent. Also all along the way there have been raspberry bushes in quantities, covered with blossom which will bye and bye develop into a lovely crop of delicious large red raspberries. Breakfasted in the little bungalow at Kotsoma, and got in soon after 4 p.m. Guason came up, and promised to bring Johnny tomorrow to be photo'd.

'Bindong' February 1902

28th Chichama. (Angami). Took Johnny's photo and then started. Found some very pretty orchids in bloom not far from the bungalow, the "Infundibulum", clusters of creamy yellow blossoms with dark red centres. Lel turned off 3½ miles out to visit his Signaling party at Tesnakotsama, and sent a message in to Tolley for one or two needs to meet us. Breakfast had been ordered "half way", the whole march being 13 miles, but for 9½ miles I hunted with an aching, longing void within, before I found it, only 3½ miles from the end of the march. Here the Dak with papers and a letter from Lady Hume met me, and I sat for an hour, in a pretty corner of the Forest till Lel came up and had his meal too. We got in fairly early and presently went out and cut some nice sticks which I had noted nearby, while Lel went and got some orchids. These latter are now a complete Coolie-load of lovely plants. The Sticks Ino Ram has since brought in trimmed up and finished in most excellent style.

March 1st Tesima. That village of Chichama as usual was most troublesome in producing coolies so we did not get off till late. It was pleasant to find breakfast ready and to sit in the shade and rest in the cool beside the bridge over the "Nerhama pani" at the bottom of that long and most trying, stoney descent. Then began the semi perpendicular ascent, which however I performed chiefly in my "Topper". Met Subadar Wazira near the top on his way out to Wokka to set matters right there and bring the Detachment into order. Got in about 3 p.m. and were met by the 3 Mirris, brought over by Japali, and who are looking positively beautiful! They certainly do Hira Sing credit in the care he has taken of them while we have been away. They are terribly out of hand though and want a lot of subduing! The little place is very tidy and neat – flowers coming on, but wants rain. It is nice to think there is no march tomorrow! In half an hour we had got photos out, cloths on tables, flowers in the vases and when we sat down to tea it was looking as pretty and home like as one could wish.

'Themakodima – Rengma Nagas'

'Gwasen and his protege J.M.'

2nd Halted. Got rather a cold. The Mirris have distinguished themselves by hunting Bannu's cat, a goat and the pony – have been beaten for each offence and tied up. Most irrepressible they are. There's a horrible wind going which gives one no peace.

3rd Halted. [4,5]

---

4.   'In the end of April 1902 your mother went to Kasauli \.... The line was now open from Dimapur to Gauhati where I saw her off on a river steamer to Calcutta'. (LWS, *Memoir.* 1926).

5.   'In mid November [1913] \.... the best doctors in Poona and Bombay attended her, she was ordered to England for a big operation (it was feared cancer), I got 2 months leave to take her home and you came down to see us off at Bombay on the P&O 'Arabia'. But we never got her home, she passed away quietly and was buried at sea two days out from Port Said on the 4th February 1914...'. (LWS, *Memoir.* 1926).

BIBLIOGRAPHY

Allen, B.C. 1980 (1905). *Naga Hills and Manipur – Socio-Economic History*. Delhi: Gian Publications.

Archer, Mildred. 1947. *Journey to Nagaland*. National Archives, MSS Eur F236/352 typed ms.

Badgley, W.F. 1875. *General Report on the Topographical Surveys of India 1874-5* in V. Elwin (ed.) *North East Frontier* 1915.

Bhattacharya, B.K. 2004 *The Brahmaputra in Assam's Economy*, in Singh, Vijay, Sharma, Nayan, Ojha, C. Shekhar P. (Eds.)*The Brahmaputra Basin Water Resources*, Springer ebooks available at: https://link.springer.com/chapter/10.1007/978-94-017-0540-0_16

Browne-Wood. 1844. *Report Extract*. Journal of the Asiatic Society.

Butler, Major John. 1855. *Travels and Adventures in the Province of Assam*. London: Smith, Elder and Co.

Butler, Captain John. 1875. *Rough Notes on the Angami Nagas and their Language*. Journal of the Asiatic Society Pt. 1, No IV.

Cawley, Mrs. 1880. *Account of the Siege of Kohima in 1879*. British Library: IOR Neg 11712/5 Typescript.

Clark, Mary Mead. 1978 (1907). *A Corner in India*. American Baptist Publication Society.

Davis, A.W. (1891). *Census of India*. Assam Vol 1 in V.Elwin (ed), *Nagas* 1969.

Elwin, Verrier. 1969. *The Nagas in the Nineteenth Century*. Bombay, London: Oxford University Press.

Elwin, Verrier. 1959. *India's North East Frontier in the Nineteenth Century*. Oxford University Press.

Evans, R.J. Professor. 2011. *The Victorians: Empire and Race*. Gresham College. Transcript available at: https://www.gresham.ac.uk › lecture › transcript › download

Grimwood, Ethel St Clair. 1891. *My Three Years in Manipur and Escape from the Recent Mutiny.* London: Richard Bentley.

Huntington, Ellsworth. 1920. *Review of History of Upper Assam, Upper Burmah and North-Eastern Frontier by L.W. Shakespear*. American Geographical Review, Vol 10, No 6, Dec 1920 pp 423-424.

Hutton, J.H. 1921. *The Angami Nagas*. London: Macmillan & Co. Ltd.

Iralu, Kaka D. 2017. *Nagaland and India: The Blood and the Tears*. Kohima, private edition.

Jacobs, Julian (ed.) 1990. *The Nagas: Hill Peoples of North East India*. London: Thames and Hudson.

Johnstone, James. 1896. *'My Experiences in Manipur and the Naga Hills'* London: Sampson Low, Marston and Company

Kennedy, Lieutenant W.M. Offg. Deputy Commissioner Naga Hills. 1901. *General Administration Report of the Naga Hills District for 1900-1901*. Nagaland State Archives; typescript.

Kennedy, Lieutenant W.M. Offg. Deputy Commissioner Naga Hills. 1900. *Tour diary for July 1900*. Nagaland State Archives; typescript.

Mackenzie, Alexander. 1979 (1884) *The North East Frontier of India*. Mittal Publications, Delhi. (reprint).

Macmillan, Margaret. 2018. *Women of the Raj*. London: Thames and Hudson.

Maitland, Captain P.J. 1880. *Detailed report on the Naga Hills Expedition of 1879-80. Simla: Intelligence Branch, QMG's Dept.* British Library: IOR/L/MIL/17/18/24.

Misra, Sanghamitra. 1998. *The Nature of Colonial Intervention in the Naga Hills, 1840-1880.* Economic and Political Weekly.

Monahan, F.J. Secretary to the Chief Commissioner for Assam. 1904. *Letter to Government of India, Home Department* (on subject of Mr. Tolley). British Library: IOR typescript of 11 April.

Oppitz, Michael, Alban von Stockhausen, Marion Wettstein and Thomas Kaiser (eds.) 2008. *Naga Identities; Changing local cultures in the Northeast of India.* Gent: Snoek Publishers.

Reid, Sir Robert. 1983 (1942). *History of the Frontier Areas Bordering on Assam (from 1883-1941).* Delhi: Eastern Publishing House.

Reuters report. 1923. *Indian Colonel Murdered. Tragedy in a Train.* The Register, Adelaide, South Australia, 26 Sep available at: https://trove.nla.gov.au/newspaper/article/65047073

Sema, Dr. Piketo. 1991. *British Policy and Administration in Nagaland 1881-1947.* Delhi, Scholar Publishing House.

Shakespear, John, Lieutenant Colonel 1929. *Lushai Reminiscences, Chapter VII 1892-1896*, Assam Review, Vol 2, No 5, July 1929.

Shakespear, L.W. 1929. *History of the Assam Rifles.* London: Macmillan & Co. Ltd.

Shakespear, L.W. 1914. *History of Upper Assam, Upper Burmah and North-Eastern Frontier.* London: Macmillan & Co. Ltd.

Shakespear, L.W. 1926. '*Renascentur*' (memoir written to his son). Unpublished ms.

Soppit, C.A. 1885. *A Short Account of the Kachcha Naga (Empeo) Tribes in the North Cachar Hills.* in V. Elwin (ed), *Nagas* 1969.

Stockhausen, Alban von. 2014. *Imag(in)ing The Nagas.* Stuttgart: Arnoldsche Art Publishers.

Van Ham, Peter and Saul, Jamie. 2008. *Expedition Naga*. ACC Editions.

Williamson, Noel. 1902. *Tour Diary of Mr. Noel Williamson Sub-divisional Officer Mokokchung, 1 and 2 August.* Nagaland State Archives: Manuscript.

Woods, Captain A.E. 1900. *Diaries of the D.C. Naga Hills for the months of January and February 1900.* Nagaland State Archives.

Woodthorpe, R.G. 1882. *Notes on the Wild Tribes Inhabiting the So-Called Naga Hills on our North-East Frontier of India Pt.II*, Journal of the Anthropological Institute of Great Britain and Ireland Vol XI.

Woodthorpe, R.G. 1876. *Letter to Captain W.F. Badgley*, in Elwin (ed.) *The Nagas*. 1969.

CONSTANCE MACKWORTH SHAKESPEAR – A SHORT BIOGRAPHY

Born in England in October 1851, Constance Biddulph was the daughter of the rector of Hampton Bishop in Herefordshire. Her two elder brothers went out to India, and she followed them in 1875 – why and with whom is not known, for her father died in Lima when she was four, and she lost her mother before she was 20. It seems probable that she joined her brother Tom and his wife Lil. She was close to them throughout her life.

Connie first met Leslie Shakespear (LWS) in India in 1883 and became engaged a year later, a match vigorously opposed by her family. At 24, her suitor was much younger. They married quietly 18 months later in Bolarum; her two brothers and three or four others attended. Missing a train meant they spent their first night together in Secunderabad station. The next day they returned to Belgaum on a ballast train with a 3rd class carriage, provided especially for them, attached.

Well connected, she twice wrote to the Commander-in-Chief, Sir Frederick Roberts, to get her husband into the 2nd Goorkhas, a regiment on which he'd set his heart. Her health failed her often, and two years after their marriage, the couple lost their first-born to dysentery. She returned to England more than once for health reasons and on other occasions to see Wyn, their only child. After years of enmity with her mother-in-law, they eventually became friends.

Accomplished in music, singing, drawing, watercolours, horse-riding and shooting (renowned as a good shot), she also assisted her husband in passing exams and writing his books. She enjoyed regimental life in Dehra Dun, where they spent many years and was in tears when LWS handed over his battalion command. She was proud of two unusual farewell gifts: a diamond and gold pendant with regimental crest given her by the officers of the regiment and a gold bracelet from the Indian officers and families of the Naga Hills Military Police battalion. Unlike her husband, she looked forward to a retired life in England. However, after 28 years of marriage and 39 years in India, this was not to be. Diagnosed with cancer, she 'passed away quietly and was buried at sea two days out from Port Said' in February 1914.

EDITOR'S NOTE

Connie's Diary came to me, a great grandson, through the family. Turning her two notebooks into a publication has only come about through the strong support of all the staff of the *Highland Institute* and *Highlander* for which I am most grateful. I would like to thank in particular Michael Heneise for his interest and enthusiasm since we first met, as well as Edward Moon-Little, Arkotong Longkumer, Catriona Child, Aditya Kiran Kakati, Rokovor Vihienuo and Alina Ronghangpi for their help in bringing Connie's diary to press.

My thanks also to the Director of the Nagaland State Archive for access to tour diaries, to Morkor Korley and Sue Maycock for their detailed comments as careful readers of the diary, and to A. Sentiyula for her kind foreword. Thanks too to John Butler of PhotoValet London for many of the scans made for the book.

Should any reader have comments or enquiries these can be made at the *Highland Institute* website at www.highlandinstitute.org/highlander/diaryofconnieshakespear. Also available there are the original unedited digital version of the diary and photographs which feature in it.

Nigel Shakespear

www.ingramcontent.com/pod-product-compliance
Lightning Source LLC
Chambersburg PA
CBHW042343300426
44109CB00049B/2825